INVASIONS
OF
PRIVACY

Cheers,
Marian Christy

INVASIONS
OF
PRIVACY

notes from a celebrity journalist

MARIAN CHRISTY

author of the nationally syndicated column "Conversations"

ADDISON-WESLEY PUBLISHING COMPANY
Reading, Massachusetts • Menlo Park, California
Wokingham, Berkshire • Amsterdam • Don Mills, Ontario • Sydney

Library of Congress Cataloging in Publication Data

Christy, Marian.
　Invasions of privacy.

　1. Christy, Marian.　2. Journalists—United States—
Biography.　3. Interviewing (Journalism)　I. Title.
PN4874.C517A34 1984　　070'.92'4 [B]　　84-10999
ISBN 0-201-10336-2

Cover design by Jean De Poian
Set in 11 point Garamond Book by Techna Type, Inc., York, PA
ABCDEFGHIJ-AL-8654

iv

for
ANNA SABA CHRISTY

SPECIAL THANKS TO:

ANN BUCHWALD, my agent and friend

TOM WINSHIP, *Globe* editor, who kindly gave me permission to juggle two jobs

MATT STORIN, managing editor, who always encouraged me

MICHAEL JANEWAY, managing editor of the Sunday *Globe*

CINDY SMITH, assistant managing editor of Living Arts

QUINNIE MCCRAY, assistant, Living Arts

THERESA BURNS, my Addison-Wesley editor

DOE COOVER and ANN DILWORTH, my Addison-Wesley support system, and

JOAN P. ROY, my typist

CONTENTS

INVASIONS
OF
PRIVACY

PROLOGUE

OPPORTUNITY doesn't present itself when you're ready to make the most of it. It appears before you unannounced and can disappear fast. There is a mystery to opportunity. You don't know for sure how it's going to turn out, which can be tantalizing because it challenges you to use your inner eye, your imagination, envision the end product at its best.

When I first started scribbling notes for this book, I wrote mainly about the celebrities I interviewed, the inside stories of intimate encounters that never found their way into the *Globe* during my nineteen years there. My publishing editors, having insight, insisted on knowing more. When I held back, they accused me, in the most friendly way, of being secretive. They made it sound like a dreadful fault! Slowly, I edged out of my shell and started scribbling my feelings about the "how" of my career, the "how" of confrontational interviews with the privileged. I began describing the specifics of the exchange of great intimacies that became the printed words under my by-line. The same editors accused me of putting interviewees on the hot seat without knowing exactly what that felt like. They wanted to know more about how *I* felt during those interviews.

Because I am a print journalist and am not part of the television world, I ignored the fact that I was, and am, the other half of the interview process. I was so lost in the role of journalist that I forgot myself. And then I realized that I almost believed those newspaper editors who used to tell me to stay out of my stories, to be uninvolved. When I came to grips with that I knew it wouldn't satisfy me— I wanted to be heard and *seen*. I had never *observed* an interview. I *felt* it. I also knew the only way to be more than a by-line was to step away from myself and, in a detached way, introduce myself. I had never done this before in my life, not even with friends. I had always thought people should discover one another gradually, a theory that controlled my interview approach, which was, and still is: tell me everything. I ended up at times interviewing myself.

At first I did this shyly, with the notion that, in the end, I was going to be sorry. The first draft of my working manuscript was written in the third person, "she." My editors casually mentioned that if I was more comfortable with approaching the story of my interviews that way, fine; in the final manuscript each "she" would be replaced with "I" anyway. It was at this point that I admitted to myself that my interviewing was a personal story, and all the editing in the world wasn't going to change the situation to describe a smooth ride to the top. I changed each "she" to "I" myself. My editors applauded. And then they asked more personal questions, more probing ones, questions they insisted I and I alone must answer. They turned the tables on me, approaching me the way I approached the people I interview—kindly, but with the attitude that there are no holds barred.

It was then that I understood that the pain and pleasures of my career and my life were my most valuable experiences, my own personal barometer of the art of living. This was the very thing that I could measure against other people, and vice versa. When I began to see the real value of my experiences, it was I who changed the pronoun.

A metamorphosis doesn't happen easily. There is a great risk to change. I also know that, without risk, there is no success. Every success involves a kind of stretching, a self-maximization, a curiosity to see how far you can take yourself. All of the people I have interviewed have taken risks, gambled on themselves. And all of them are successful—though not always in the way you might think.

Now I tend to see opportunity as a bigger arena, the chance to pioneer a new kind of newspapering. For me, the opportunity is, I think, to prove to the toughest, most stubborn editors that there's more than one way to tell a story, that revealment doesn't have to be a classic cut-up portrait, that the best stories are collaborations. As I have emerged out of my own shell, I have insisted that the persons I interview do the same thing. The joy is that they have reached out willingly, met me on my own ground. At last I am experiencing the joy of mutuality. I am less alone because of it. My mother called it "taking opportunity of opportunity, ready or not." What I discovered was that I was ready.

CONVERSATIONS

ON A STARRY Roman summer night, at about nine o'clock, in a searingly spotlighted building somewhere near the Spanish Steps, a human traffic jam was occurring. The rest of Via Gregoriana was steeped in blackness, except in front of No. 24, which was lit like a center stage.

Elaborately gowned women and tuxedoed men emerged slowly from a small string of chauffeured cars and smiled on cue as the legendary Italian paparazzi aimed cameras at them like guns. The shot terminated the facade of gentility. Despite their crisp formal clothes, these same people visibly gritted their teeth and elbowed their way into the mad crush of writhing bodies clogging the doorway.

The name of the game was Getting Inside, onto hallowed ground, no easy matter if the name on your invitation didn't match exactly the name on the "list," the one being checked at the door by pretty women dressed in black and backed by discreet bouncers, also wearing black. The door staff, pretending to be oblivious to the madness, were pseudopolice, hired for their ability to spot gate crashers or, worse, spies and thieves who might infiltrate the building.

Judging from the intensity of the hour-long entrance hysteria, you'd hardly guess this was only opening night of the 1967 semiannual couture collection of Valentino, the trendy Italian couturier whose designs were favored by the then-world's most prominent fashion consumer, Jacqueline Kennedy Onassis. Jackie had made Oleg Cassini her "official" White House designer. But now her heart belonged to Valentino. This vital sentiment, headlined by the international press, fueled the flame of interest to epidemic. Of course Valentino probably had already gone to New York and shown Jackie privately what everyone was fighting to see now, supposedly before she did.

Prior to the onslaught of the feminist movement, before the fickleness of fashion became its very detriment, when designers were indeed divine dictators, getting a seat to the couture opening of a Valentino collection was a life or death matter. The showings attracted a motley group, a mixture of so-called beautiful people and rough-and-tumble cameramen and international reporters who sometimes smelled sourly of marijuana. Often these disparate types were forced to sit side-by-side, especially if the reporter had a "reputation," Which is to say, wrote fluff reports blatantly favorable to the designer.

Valentino was then the undisputed king of Italian fashion, one of the few influentials who seemed to have the uncanny power to convince women to throw out everything in their closets every six months and begin again. Valentino was the talented upstart who upstaged his Paris counterparts, a sudden nouveau millionaire whose elegant private home boasted at least one room designed like the paisley tent of an oil-rich sheik.

The *Boston Globe* wanted a series of first-hand stories on these breathless frivolities. And there I was, caught in the Valentino doorway squash, trying to get into the inner sanctum for the first time. Later I would discover that the salon had no air conditioning, that the closely placed seats touched each other and so did the thighs of the people sitting on them, that the Japanese segment always used hand-size whirring plastic fans, soon to be the rage of Rome and Paris, "gifts" given to the press at the door. I also discovered why many people held lavender-scented handkerchiefs to their noses. Not everyone used Dial. Smoking was allowed. There were no fire laws.

Valentino, master showman, used a trick all major European designers still use to create the impression of frenzied demand. Three times as many guests as could possibly be accommodated were invited to the small salons. A circus atmosphere quickly developed. It looked as if the invitations were in enormous demand. For some, they were. Fist fights would develop at the door, mad scuffles over one seat assigned to two people. Name calling was frequent. You didn't need to understand any foreign language being spoken in the heat of passion for fashion.

If you were a beginner, as I was in the late sixties, you were relegated automatically to the back row at Valentino. Season by season, year by year, you moved forward if—*big* if,—your reports were "approved." The less critical you were, the better your chances of advancing to the front. It always helped to have New York connections, people who would execute well-placed telephone calls to authenticate your power.

In Valentino's case, approval had to come from his trusted personal companion, a handsome young man named Giancarlo Giammetti, one of the many European fashion gods who operated a kind of caste system. I knew all this. But I wasn't worried. Didn't I have an invitation in my hand? I was content to accept the back row, jammed against the salon wall. It would be satisfying just to peek at the runway through the blurred heads of the people in the front rows.

But Giancarlo, wearing a torso-tracing Valentino tuxedo with extended shoulders and a nipped-in waist, told me there was no seat, that I wasn't on the official list. From an expression of bored weariness, he asked: "What is the

Boston Globe anyway?" Only he pronounced Globe, "glub."
No amount of arguing or pleading could get Giancarlo to
change his mind. He had given my precious seat away but
I refused to budge from the outer salon. He ignored me.

Just before the show started, when the blinding runway lights snapped on, when the audience chatter suddenly
disintegrated into high-strung silence, Giancarlo put a chair
in front of the main salon doorway, blocking it. He whispered a dare: Would I like to observe the eighty-minute
show from somewhere up on high, standing on that chair?

It was a social embarrassment. A career insult. But I
had come all the way to Rome to cover the show. The
minute I hopped up on the chair, Giancarlo also encouraged a wispy Japanese reporter, a tiny woman who weighed
ninety pounds and had a coal-colored Buster Brown hair-
cut, to join me on the chair. She did. And there we were,
two foreigners from homes half a world apart, sharing the
same precarious vantage point at the famous Valentino salon in Rome.

The standing room only development was a blessing
in disguise. It forced on me an overview of the entire
presentation. The jammed audience. The Kleig-lighted runway. The salon studded with gilt chairs with wine velvet
seats. By necessity, I was frozen there, unable to move.

Runway goings-on were marvelous theatre and I got
lost in the silliness of the plot. Glamorous women, me-
ticulously painted to look like living department store
dummies, wore blank expressions, fantastic clothes and
dripped Bulgari jewels. Sometimes they leaned languish-
ingly against men wearing impeccable suits. But the pretty
men always seemed to gaze in another direction, as if they
were bored to distraction by the glory of their female
counterparts. It was a fascinating caricature, something totally separate from the real world of men and women.

On that chair, perched like a nervous bird on the
rafters, I decided to write a sidebar story to the big one:
what Valentino enthusiasts wore to a Valentino show, (mostly

"old" Valentinos, a loyalist salute to the man-of-the-hour).

Then I spotted Princess Luciana Pignatelli, who later became the Camay soap ads model on American television. She was wearing a caftan. Caftans were then considered nothing more than fancy lingerie never meant to go public. She had dared to break the rule of formality and *not* dress in regular evening clothes. I wrote the story, dictated it into a *Boston Globe* Dictaphone by static-studded trans-oceanic telephone and next day the report appeared exactly as I had written it. Except for one word change. It said, under my by-line, that Princess Pignatelli, a fashion rebel, had arrived at the Valentino salon wearing not a caftan but, of all things, an afghan.

$$\Diamond$$

THAT WAS MY baptism into the world of haute couture. I had arrived there on a fluke, having been a beginning reporter in the Boston bureau of *Women's Wear Daily,* taking whatever assignment came from New York headquarters via teletype. Mostly I got "survey" work, something reporters of substance avoided gingerly. Surveys required that you telephone key retail executives, read canned questions about sales trends from mimeographed memos, and return brief quotes to New York where they would be assembled into national surveys. This was not by-line work.

In 1964, a survey clicked on the teletype. The Boston bureau chief instructed the teletype operator to flash back the message to New York that this would have to wait for the "return of Christy." I was out to lunch. The operator was also in a hurry to go out to lunch. In her haste, she inadvertently sent back the message that the assignment would have to wait for the "return of Christ."

The message immediately caused a big uproar at Fairchild headquarters. Gossip then was that John Fairchild, the publishing giant whose family owned the Fairchild Publications empire, which included *Women's Wear,* would tease his then-executive editor, James Brady, who later became a *Harper's Bazaar* publisher and author. Did Fairchild Publications *really* have a Christ, as in Jesus, on its staff? Fairchild and Brady, to whom fashion was a religion, were amused enough to ferret me out, give me a devilish assignment, a bad joke.

Women's Wear and Oleg Cassini, the designer, were feuding badly, a fact I didn't know. Each wanted nothing to do with the other. "Christ" was told to get an interview with Cassini, who was doing a Saturday afternoon fashion show in Boston.

After the show, I went to Cassini's suite. Tea was being served to the press assembled there. Joan Kennedy, a friend of Cassini's, was at his side. The instant I identified myself as a *Women's Wear Daily* reporter Cassini became loud and angry. "Leave this suite immediately," Cassini bellowed, and I thought he was talking to someone else. But he said he wanted nothing to do with *me* and that the press conference would not continue until I left. I was flabbergasted. I called *Women's Wear* headquarters in New York, got an old-timer editor on the phone who told me not to worry, to write something "short and punchy" about Cassini's temper tantrum. He congratulated me for getting as far as Cassini's suite. He said he was sure that Fairchild would be pleased that I had such an interesting "item" about Cassini. The story, not more than 500 words, appeared in a black box—like an old-fashioned funeral announcement—on page 1 the following Monday.

I thought my career was over but, after that, James Brady begin to give me better assignments: What kinds of women did Harvard men pursue and why? A talk with Julie Andrews on location at Sturbridge Village. Interviews with Bill Blass, a rising young designer, and one of the Ferragamos of shoe fame. I never heard from Fairchild nor had anything to do with him. But James Brady himself wrote me notes of encouragement. Frequently he brought me to

New York headquarters to "get the feel" of newspapering. He urged me to linger in the shadows of the women who edited the pages, to absorb their action and style, to listen and to watch. One day I knew I could be sitting where they were now.

The *Boston Globe* noticed my *Women's Wear* layouts, which were getting bigger and splashier. Late in the winter of 1965, I got a hurried telephone call from the *Globe* from Sumner Barton, who said that Tom Winship, the *Globe's* new editor, was hunting for a fashion editor and my work had been called to his attention. Would I come in for an interview? I didn't need a job. I had one. And that's the attitude with which I went to the *Globe* several weeks later. I was, in fact, uncharacteristically flip. When Barton suggested I sit down, I said I couldn't because his chair was laden with cigar ashes. He gallantly flourished a rag from his desk and cleaned the chair with a dramatic sweep. Between us there was a sense of mutual mischief tempered with respect. Before I left the *Globe* building, I met Winship for the first time. He was polite and terse, silent but observant. He asked no questions, made no comment. But Barton shook my hand in a lingering way and smiled in approval. He said he'd be calling me.

In April 1965, Sumner Barton offered me the job as *Globe* fashion editor, $165 a week, $30 more than *Women's Wear*. When I gave my resignation, the bureau chief offered to equal, even top, the *Globe's* offer. He told me that I could be assigned immediately to the New York office to be a page editor. It was a last-minute temptation. The *Globe* had insisted I accept a six-month probation. They wanted to see if they liked my work and if, indeed, they liked *me*. I decided the *Globe* offered better long-term opportunity. The *Globe* had promised the European assignments.

The great twist of irony is that at the European couture showings, the *Women's Wear* contingent is considered holy. *Women's Wear* influences the retailing trade with its cri-

tiques of what's good, trendy, and what isn't. A good or
bad review could, like Broadway, make or break a show
and a designer. *Women's Wear* staffers got front-row seats
and reverential treatment. If I had stayed at *Women's Wear,*
and been assigned to Europe, I would not be standing on
a chair. I would be up front rather than on-high.

◇

THE BIG-NAME Paris shows I covered for the *Globe* from
1967 to 1974 were stifling repeats of the Valentino performance. Only the characters would change. The frail,
wispy Chanel, growing old before our eyes, sat at the top
of the winding staircase of her salon, directly under a giant
portrait of her young self, and scrutinized the mannequins
who modeled the same type Chanel suits she had worn
decades earlier in her portrait, and like the one she was
then wearing.

Pierre Cardin was embroiled in the space age, producing weird costumes for imagined moon travel. Only
some of the lunar skirts were so skin-tight that models
maneuvered the stage only with the most careful mincing.
At Courrèges, everyone wore white sportswear and white
shoes, even Courrèges himself. Since the utilitarian salon
was also all white, you'd swear you were in a hospital until
braless models appeared on the dime-size stage and began
to undulate pornographically to piped-in rock music.

At Christian Dior, the press with the least impressive
credentials was seated in a mass of bodies on the long,
winding staircases leading to the main salon. These unfor-
tunates, myself among them but lucky enough to be seated
on a chair, watched the show at eye level. What they saw
were the hemlines of stringbean mannequins flitting by in
mink coats dyed outrageous rainbow colors. Risqué jokes
were quietly cracked on those Dior stairs, jokes about models
who wore furs only over tights, jokes about being able to

look up and see more than was intended. Giggles were often disguised as coughs. The Dior show caused the most strident speculation among small cliques of reporters who later gathered at tiny neighborhood cafes along the Avenue Montaigne to compare notes, to share a *croque monsieur* sandwich and a bottle of beaujolais and, most important, to play an intriguing if outrageous guessing game. Which Dior models were really men disguised as women, their beards shaved off, their legs waxed? Was it so-and-so? No, no! It was ...

Covering an Yves Saint Laurent show was the most frustrating. Desirable front-row seats were always reserved for special friends from *Vogue* and *Harper's Bazaar* and clients like Paloma Picasso and Catherine Deneuve, who drew international photographers like flies. Seats, not the cushiony variety, were attached in immovable rows so that every viewer was forced to remain stationary, to follow the fashion mannequin's antics the way people watch a tennis match.

Once I dared to squirm, to sit at an awkward angle to see the models better through many heads blocking my view. A Saint Laurent *vendeuse*, the wife of a rich French-man, shot out of the nearby dressing room and swiftly, expertly moved me bodily into position. She had spied me while peering through the velvet curtains of the dressing room. As if I were a naughty child caught misbehaving, she sat me at strict attention. Shoulders square! Face forward! I flushed in fury, the same as if I had been slapped. I sat frozen in the militaristic, upright posture into which I had been set, partly from stunned reaction, partly from self-control.

The primitive desire to retaliate, even verbally, was immediately cancelled by a very practical fear. It was a bad seat but it was better than standing on a chair. I could lose my place! This woman, who was wearing large diamond earrings, Giancarlo's Parisian counterpart, had the upper hand. She policed the chaos of a couture opening with flamboyant gestures of law-and-order from which the front row celebrities-in-attention were, of course, exempt. Her job was to restrain the socially inferior press by domination, the press being the very people who would write the stories that fanned the fame of her employers. What always puzzled me was the timorousness of the international fashion press, the way reporters accepted the uncivilized reception they were given, as if bad manners were their due. There seemed to be no dignity to newspapering.

The jolt from the strong hand of the *vendeuse* brought up another issue that bothered me about this brand of journalism. Just as I was compelled to *sit* a certain way, it was clear to me that I was expected to *write* a certain way, the usual boring stories about changing necklines, waistlines, hemlines. The woman, a symbol of the Paris attitude toward the press, had made herself clearly understood. She made me realize that being allowed entry into a Paris salon at showtime was not necessarily equal to being ushered through the gates of heaven. This enlightenment didn't hit me entirely in one fell swoop. But at that moment I began caring much less about pleasing the designer with praise pieces and more about telling the reader what was *really* happening in the rarefied atmosphere called a "salon," a place I likened in print to a saloon.

I had never been a breathless fashion worshipper who considered couturiers gods. They were talented tailors. They were not inventing a cure for cancer. They were creating *clothes.* But designers are also clever communicators who make social statements through models, their live visuals. Couture shows don't have commentators, people to explain what's going on, the "why" of the fashions being shown. Models prance and pirouette while holding up placards with numbers, like the ones chauffeurs use at airports to pick up passengers. The numbers are for the convenience of store buyers in the audience, people who may want to order that "number" for their affluent clients back home.

Classic reporting didn't seem to be enough of a mirror to give the reader a true reflection of what was going on. Couture shows seemed to cry for translation, interpretation, opinion. I wanted to editorialize in the best, most honest sense of the word. I wanted to tell the truth not only about the clothes but about the environment, the attitude, the people, the place. I had no intention of being bitchy. I wanted to make this arena more interesting.

Covering the European fashion world, as I did every six months for seven years until 1974, was a job considered prestigious "women's work." The pages carrying my fashion reports were called "women's pages," the very same place where you could find recipes and household hints. To cover fashion was then considered the glamorous side of newspapering. If you were smart, you played the game predictably. But I thought: if you remove the by-line, you shouldn't be able to tell if the pieces were written by a man or a woman. Good journalism should be sexless, like a good painting.

My mother had always said: "If you feel a tap on your shoulder, open your eyes. It may be a message." As it turned out, the very Saint Laurent show at which I had been chastised provided me with fodder for the notion of editorializing. A stringbean model with pancake-flat breasts suddenly shot out of the dressing room. She was wearing a serious business suit over a see-through blouse worn over nothing. Was this a burlesque? If taken literally, it meant that Yves Saint Laurent, whose mother was in the audience, was advocating that chic women everywhere appear in public only one sheer veil away from nudity.

No, no. That wasn't it at all. Haute couture is a laboratory for new ideas. Saint Laurent was not advocating public near-nudity. It was poetic exaggeration to shock the eyes. Once you see the extreme overstatements, watered-down versions seem reasonable and palatable. This was the late sixties and Saint Laurent seemed to be suggesting that women's bodies should be unharnessed. It was his first bow to feminism. Bared bosoms were bedroom sanctions, portents of pillow talk. The bralessness also suggested sexual emancipation. The concept of equality in the boardroom came across when he put women in men's trouser suits that season, adding classic fedoras angled rakishly over one eye. This projected the idea of executive peerage, equal pay for equal work done by women in equal clothes. Saint Laurent seemed to be seeing women as they saw themselves in their wildest fantasies: as great career successes who also succeeded as sex goddesses. I scribbled these thoughts in my notebook.

And then Saint Laurent sent out his bride, the grand wedding gown finale that signals the end of all couture shows. Only this bride was wearing just a bikini of fresh gardenias. The audience first gasped, then went wild with applause. Saint Laurent even appeared to be sanctioning relationshhips that had nothing to do with church or the law. Maybe all this symbolism was the designer's astute vision of the New Woman, his social commentary on the times, his prediction of things to come. Saint Laurent, truly a genius, had used clothes as a method to tell his story of the future female. He had, it seemed, balanced the irrevocable but delicate link between feminism and femininity, the great female power. This was not a collection designed in an ivory tower. It had a great earthiness. Yet it was prophetically inventive.

That's the way I wrote the story, more shyly than I wanted. Maybe I would be laughed at, I thought, and criticized. I wasn't writing the way adored fashion editors write. But my mother sent the clips to me in Paris and when I saw the stories in print, the approach had a clarity. So I continued to write in that vein and I didn't get front-row seats, grand flowers in my room, or lofty invitations to great dinners with powerful people. My reward was getting an audience.

United Features Syndicate of New York picked up my stories and, in the span of two years, sold my fashion col-

umn to 104 newspapers across America. Three times, in
1966 and 1968 and 1970, I won the University of Missouri–
J. C. Penney awards for fashion journalism. The late Professor Paul Myhre told me that I had set new standards of
fashion journalism by making daring and dazzling comments on social pretentions and, he said, "trailed fashion
firsts behind me like golden confetti." It was heady stuff.
At the final black tie banquet ceremony on campus, Al
Newharth, the Gannett chain powerhouse who now pub-
lishes *USA Today,* sat next to me at the head table and told
me that I was now a part of the newspaper establishment.

My *Globe* editors seemed to agree. I was encouraged
to write frequent editorials on the follies of fashion as I
saw them. The approach seemed to make sense, to coincide
with the feminist movement of freedom from dictatorship,
even from the world of fashion. When minis emerged, I
advised women with fat knees to ignore them. When the
clumsy, depressing midis of the early seventies put hemlines on a down elevator, I said the look was ugly, that it
badly needed the refinement of an elegance that went beyond change for the sake of *change.* When blue denim hit
the Paris runways, I said glibly it had been around the
Harvard College campus for years, that an uninspired Paris
seemed to be stealing "inspiration" from American street
life. When designers put labels outside on scarfs, hip pockets, and shirtsleeves, I suggested that people wearing them
had become human billboards who ought to charge the
designers for space. I had traveled, observed, covered fashion in salons and on the streets. I felt I had earned my
opinions.

In 1972, after I had been covering European couture
for five years, the *Globe* got a letter from Paris to the effect
that I was no longer welcome to cover the couture. The
specific reason given in the letter was that I had painted
a somewhat less than *la vie en rose* picture of French
fashion.

The letter said the French organization that extended

credentials to get into the shows, La Chambre Syndicale de la Couture Parisienne, would no longer validate me. In effect, I had been thrown out. The *Globe* used its contacts in the French Embassy and French consulate to get my press card back. But first I had to confront a local French government official over lunch in Boston, a short, rotund man with a shiny bald head and a pot belly. He smoked a smelly cigar and by the end of our conversation told me that I was temporarily forgiven. But he made me understand that I must tow the line in the future, be less critical. Then the Frenchman raised his eyebrows menacingly and aimed several quick puffs at me. Our vision of each other was blurred by a deliberate, stinking smoke screen.

But I truly believed that the public should not be duped into undiscerning admiration for Paris. It should be amused by its goings-on, the fantasy of fashion. I didn't tell the French official this. I went back to Paris, validated but warned, and wrote news stories on important happenings in the salons. When I returned to Boston, I wrote separate editorials that analyzed and commented on the news.

Paris ignored this double-pronged editorial approach because I was from Boston, a town the French considered provincial. I did not represent a New York newspaper. I was syndicated in a lot of American cities and towns. But I was not national in the sense of being a household name. I had been so busy writing, I had no inkling that there was behind-the-scene trouble brewing right in Boston. I was blinded by deadlines, by the idea that this was my "time." I thought I was making a difference.

$$\Diamond$$

SERIOUS sniping began late in 1979 when one department store teamed with one specialty shop to exert pressure on the *Boston Globe* through its advertising department. Perhaps it appears to readers that fashion editors have an open ticket, that they are beyond the influence of stores, that

they don't have to pay serious editorial homage to adver-
tisers. It's not true.

Never speaking directly to me, the two retailers insisted to management that basic fashion editorials should
revolve around two kinds of reports: what stores were
carrying on their racks and features on designers making
personal appearances in those stores. Both are the basic
stuff of ads. Besides, the stores argued, I should be "selling"
fashion, not talking about its warts.

What started the ruckus were two of my opinion columns. One concerned the incoherence of skin-tight jeans
worn with strappy high-heeled evening shoes, a coarse look
that had emanated from the Paris runways. But it reminded
me of the blatantly come-hither look that European pros-
titutes use to advertise themselves. I theorized, in that
column, that it was a look not meant to be taken literally,
that it merely symbolized a new "anything goes" attitude.
I said it was Paris's way of announcing there was no single standard hemline, no one silhouette, no one standout
color of the season. "Rules" were a thing of the fashion
past. Women were free to be their own editors. I urged
that women consider it a message, not a specific look to
emulate. This made the department store executive mad.
They didn't want women to think twice about what Paris
was telling them to wear because they were selling it in
their ads.

More criticism came after a second editorial about
designer Oscar de la Renta, a man I admire enormously.
Instead of sticking to his forte, beautifully elegant clothes
bursting with ruffles, the name of one of his perfumes, he
applied his creative talent to designing or re-designing the
classic Boy Scout uniform. That seemed ridiculous to me.
Boy Scouts didn't require Oscar's couture talent. Boy Scouts
didn't need to pay more for uniforms, ostensibly because
Oscar's hand was involved. Boy Scouts didn't need a fashion
connection. At the sound of these two editorial protesta-
tions, the two retailers deemed I had gone too far. They
put serious pressure on the *Globe.* There were big exec-

utive meetings I never knew about, meetings at which my
editorial approach was voted against, and my fashion career
came to a close.

Overnight things came to a head. I was called into an
editor's office, the door was closed, and I was issued a
choice. Either approach fashion editing with heavy em-
phasis on retail promotions and localized reports *or* move
permanently into writing feature stories based on traditional question-and-answer interviews with famous people.

When I protested, not without emotion, that I did not
see myself as a merchandiser of whatever happened to be
on store racks, I was advised to cover street fashions, what
Boston people actually wore to set trends. I refused, arguing
that true Bostonians, with a few notable exceptions, are
not fashion trendsetters. They don't seem to buy clothes
for fashion as much as for value and wearability. By and
large, they have the "attic" mentality toward chic, preferring to improve their intellects rather than decorate their
bodies.

But it is this same intelligent audience that is amused
by fashion, that can see through its theatrical antics, that
is fascinated by suggested trends, that wants to know quickly
what is happening. Bostonians, like millions of people
everywhere, have a discriminating attitude toward the fashion world. That's the audience to which I had been playing
until November, 1979.

What worked for me did not seem to be working for
the *Globe*. I found myself caught between hard-fought editorial freedom and the economics of a powerful newspaper. The editor breaking the bad news to me told me to
think this over. He gave me twenty-four hours to make up
my mind.

$$\diamondsuit$$

I ALWAYS expected that great decisions are accompanied
by flashes of clarity. But a woman I greatly admire, Shirley

Hofstedler, a lawyer, a judge, President Jimmy Carter's secretary of education, once told me that when she made wrenching decisions in a court of law, there were no great moments of illumination. She proceeded on the theory that she, one fallible human being, would do the best she could with the information at hand. She said you must express yourself with a degree of confidence. You cannot wait until you are absolutely sure. I had asked her if there was a "secret" to decision-making. Her answer was starkly simple: "I accept the fact that I've made a decision and *go on.*"

I decided to leave the world of fashion and try my hand at feature stories, etc. But I felt sorry for myself. In a stand-up-and-be-counted situation, you always feel twangs of self-doubt. If you don't, you're a fool. Pain, the way you bear it, can open up the window of yourself. My pride of originality would be far more prudent in the future, because I understood myself better. My basic attitude about a new journalism had not changed. I still had my sense of creativity, my vision, my originality. No one had robbed me of my inner equipment. I wanted to take the best of me, the best of my capabilities, and apply them to a new kind of people interviews. This was not to happen overnight. For several years I went on and wrote features based on straightforward interviews. I was just coasting.

◇

I TRIED TO bolster my confidence by playing silly mind games with myself. One, in particular, worked. I pretended I was standing on a chair, just the way I had at the Valentino salon, and I imagined I was looking at an overview of what I had achieved, deciding what experiences and insights I could take with me, what could be applied in another direction. Beginnings have everything to do with attitude. Starting over begins when you say to yourself that what's finished is finished.

Out of the pain, out of what looked like major career rejection, something unexpected, something good, had happened to me in terms of my own feelings and emotions. I became more sensitive than ever. That sensitivity made me more susceptible to subtle nuances within myself and within others. I felt more deeply and that helped me to see others more clearly. The pain of rejection had actually honed my emotions to give me a sharper perspective.

And that's when I understood there's a good side to vulnerability, a positive one. Vulnerability makes you receptive; it opens up your channels of curiosity. You begin to seek answers to questions you didn't know you had. Instead of getting behind the facade of fashion, I would penetrate the facade of people. What got me thinking about a new approach to interviews, conversations with a new two-way twist, was the notion that other people's feelings were akin to mine, akin to everybody's. Is there a soul among us who doesn't know what it is to get up after you've been knocked down? I also knew that no one tells anybody everything. People like to keep a piece of themselves to themselves. But if I were to offer a piece of myself to another person, how would that person react?

There was surely something connecting us all. The word "oneness" stuck in my head. At first, we don't admit it. We tend to flaunt our differentness. That is only the veneer of our real selves, the mask that hides us, protects us. The unity of our feelings is the glue that holds all of us together. Only we are reluctant to expose those feelings because we are afraid of being hurt. We wait until someone else makes the first move, speaks from the heart and gut. Then we say: "Oh, yes! I know *that* feeling." The first person, deeply human stories I wanted to explore were *how* the person knows, the experiences, the motivations, the failures, and the successes involved in those feelings. I also had to face up to the fact that I couldn't get these stories until I came out of my shell first, offered my own feelings as an invitation to exchange feelings that would appear in print. I was excited by the idea of this kind of interviewing.

◇

MONTHS LATER I expressed my "oneness" theory to one of my editors. No one would understand what I was talking about, he said. Regular twice-weekly celebrity columns couldn't possibly have such a specific connective tissue. On a sustained basis it would be impossible to get famous people to talk about intimate feelings. He also criticized me for being insatiably ambitious, a trait he likened to being "greedy." I got the very same feeling I had in Paris, when the *vendeuse* told me I had to sit a certain way by actually pushing me into position.

So I decided that on my own, when the opportunity arose, I would experiment, see if I could get people to expose their gut feelings, talk to me about the details of survival, about pain and triumph, about setbacks and struggles. I hoped that readers would understand my approach, would say: I know how that feels. I also believed that people could inspire one another. It would be a subtle advice column in reverse, the advice coming from a celebrity who had lived out a crisis and told how.

The only trouble with this approach is that you cannot press a button and immediately expect a coherent outpouring of emotional disclosures. People don't tell you what's going on in their hearts and their heads in one beautiful spurt. They hedge. They pussyfoot around the truth. The "Conversations," as they came to be called, come in painstaking bits and pieces, like a puzzle to be assembled into a complete word picture later. I knew that the interviews would have to be two-way streets between the person being interviewed and me. The only way to conjure up the best quotes would be to share experiences and refine and distill them togther. The approach would have to be one of mutuality, and I would have to set that mood.

And then I made this discovery: only the most successful people talk about their setbacks and failures, because they've overcome them. Failures are the milestones of their lives, negatives turned around. People enmired in continuing failure or mediocrity blur with the crowd, become indistinguishable. They haven't dared to start over, try again, establish a new beginning. That was my connection to the people I interviewed.

I also began to see how little the long run matters. You don't eat, sleep, or love in the long run. You do it every day. And the days, all equal short runs, blur into the long run, extending your path and your vision. I decided to go step by step, approaching each interview as an interpersonal encounter. Between us, we began to peel away the layers that mask us from each other. It was a great sharing.

I tested this new kind of interviewing for the first time on a cold January day in 1982.

$$\Diamond$$

HARSH NOONTIME shadows danced in and out of the Salad Boat, a simple neighborhood restaurant in Lansdowne, Pennsylvania. I brooded that maybe the old woman, a stranger, wouldn't come at all. She was already a half hour late.

When the second cup of black coffee arrived, so did Anna Hauptmann, age eighty-two, leaning trustingly on the arm of a young Los Angeles lawyer, Robert R. Bryan. The woman was garbed in neat, well-worn widow's clothes. She had dressed like this for forty-seven years.

Mrs. Hauptmann moved in slow motion, easing gently into a booth, whispering an order for a bowl of chowder that she never touched. Her bony hands unconsciously twisted a white lace handkerchief. Her life had been hard. Her half-lidded glance was simultaneously penetrating and sleepy but those sad eyes never spilled tears. There were none left.

Anna Hauptmann was not a celebrity except by long-ago association that ended abruptly in 1935 when her husband, Bruno Richard Hauptmann, was electrocuted in New Jersey after being convicted of kidnapping and murdering the Charles Lindbergh baby. Headlines around the world proclaimed it the trial of the century. In a way, Mrs. Hauptmann died when her husband died. She had proclaimed his innocence, swearing over and over again they were together the night of the murder, together in the Bronx, not New Jersey.

She was largely ignored. Now in the final chapter of life, she gamely stepped out of a self-imposed shell of silence. After forty-seven years, she wanted to clear her late husband's name, reverse history, explain her feelings to the world. It was a courageous step. She was old, physically weak, her life was fading. She had no assurance that anyone would care or understand. I wanted to hear her story.

Even though the sensational Hauptmann case had been re-opened recently, I did not go to Lansdowne, Pennsylvania, as an investigative reporter. I was not there to pass judgment on whether or not Hauptmann was framed, as Anna and her lawyer, Bryan, were claiming. I was not suspicious that her late husband had been the victim of illegal searches, of bodily assaults, of a litany of false testimony. I did not go to meet Mrs. Hauptmann to be convinced the guilty verdict should have been not guilty.

Anna Hauptmann spoke in a faint German accent. Her tongue lingered lovingly on the word "truth." "The truth," she said, "is stronger than anything else." She was deeply motivated by the power of truth, she was gambling on it, fortressing it with simple words like "faith" and "love."

Her lawyer had, by then, filed a $100-million suit in

New Jersey to establish Hauptmann's innocence, once and
for all. He was seeking a jury trial to absolve Hauptmann.
He wanted to open for inspection 90,000 pieces of evidence in custody. At the mention of $100 million, the old
woman sat up straight and interrupted. She'd take $1 if the
court would enter an order that Hauptmann was wrongly
executed.

Success, as she saw it, was vindication, not cash. Her
future on earth was limited. Money was of no value.

"One day after thinking, 'No, I can't go on,' I asked
God to guide me," she told me. "To tell me what to do. I
went to sleep thinking how God forgave his persecutors
and from then on I was like a different person. But I had
misgivings. Should I start now? At this age? But I realize
that I could not die without doing anything. So I said: *I'm
going to do it.*'"

Mrs. Hauptmann laid her vulnerabilities before me,
parading "mistakes," calling herself "dumb." Her marriage
was a star-crossed love affair. Yet she insisted that love was
the world's greatest force, something worth fighting for.

On the plane I realized this hadn't been an interview
at all, not in the classic newspaper sense. It was a moving
encounter. We had exchanged thoughts and feelings, reacted to each other as caring friends although we had never
met before. I didn't have a tape recorder. I never use one,
convinced that the sheer technology of machines interferes
with the humanness of two people extending themselves
to each other. Eavesdroppers annoy me. A tape recorder
is an eavesdropper. Mrs. Hauptmann accepted my simple
note-taking. We had trusted one another.

On the plane ride back, I wrote the story longhand in
a new format—a short prologue followed by the old woman
speaking for herself. My editor was pleased and ran the
piece as is. Right after it was published, Mrs. Hauptmann's
lawyer called to tell me the story was accurate and moving.
He asked if I'd consider writing Mrs. Hauptmann's story in
book form. She wanted me to do it. I was grateful but I

knew what I really wanted to do: make this into a new kind of interview journalism.

People who agree to be interviewed by the press usually have an adversary relationship with journalists. There is a feeling of natural distrust. Quotes can easily be twisted and reflect in a maligning way. People who usually talk to the press do so for a reason. They are promoting themselves for one reason or another. They want to use the press for their own good. It is very hard for a journalist not to feel used and become defensive and suspicious.

I began to tell the people I was interviewing in advance that I was not out for gossip, that I thought the interview process could be a real sharing of feelings that readers everywhere could understand. The reaction from people I interviewed was generally positive, open. That's how I began to excise exciting quotes. I could get people to tell me the unexpected, the surprising, because I threw in some of my own ideas and feelings. The more they told me, the more readers said they understood because it was like looking in a mirror.

Since meeting Mrs. Hauptmann in 1982, I began to dig deeper in my interviews, but with gentleness and compassion. Over and over, I heard stories that paralleled my feelings, everybody's feelings. I was invading people's privacy with their cooperation. I did not stalk them. I did not hound. You can't force cordiality and reciprocity. Even the most pointed questions are posed softly, tenderly. I came to the interview as a friend, guiding it, keeping it on track, adding ideas to it, subtracting powerful quotes.

I wanted to go further, much further, with those quotes. I strung them together as if the interviewee were talking directly, emotionally, to the reader without interruption, explanation, or judgment from me. There were no regular first-person interview columns in American newspapers at that time. Frequently cut-and-dried tape recorded interviews appeared. I suggested the column be called "Conversations," a word that suggests two people talking heart-to-heart and, after a short prologue setting the scene, the person would speak for himself or herself. The mail began to pour in. The telephones started ringing. People who didn't know me except by name were asking for more stories in this new direction.

The sense of mutuality multiplied many times. I became the recipient of attitudes as original as the fingerprints of the people I interviewed. Interviews became rich encounters, the real education of my life. Slowly but surely, out of the events that had begun with my standing on the Valentino chair and which ended when I relinquished my *Globe* fashion chair, I had carved a new place. This was my best, most satisfying writing.

It was October, 1981. Like my other *Globe* editor, Tom Winship didn't think the empathy approach would work. Once in awhile, Winship said, people would open up *if,* as he put it, I "got lucky." He told me not to be too disappointed if I failed. He asked me if I could admit to failure. I never answered him. All I know for sure is what he finally said: "I run a loose ship. Try it for a year. If you pull this thing off, we'll meet in exactly one year to see where you can go from there."

◇

NINETEEN EIGHTY-TWO was a wonderfully productive year. So was 1983. I wrote twice-weekly first-person stories about famous people from a cross-section of lifestyles, people who shared intimate feelings with me and allowed me to share mine with them. I had proven to my editors, and to myself, that mutuality works, that a columnist can be involved and involving, that sensational stories don't have to be bitchy, that it's possible to invade people's privacy and not hurt them.

BEATING
THE ODDS

MY FATHER WAS a successful and handsome restaurateur who never finished grade school, a fanatical historian who knew the dates and details of every war ever fought. He was a self-taught mathematical wizard who could draw magnificent sketches of ancient sailing vessels, an art sophisticate who frequented New York auctions and collected fine cloisonné and Chinese jardinieres. He was also a campaign strategist, a man with a surprising grip of commercial law. One of his old cronies was House Speaker Tip O'Neill. His canny advice was sought by many neighborhood politicians. So was his money. He seemed to give generously of both.

Sometimes neighborhood police officials, all Irishmen except for one Italian detective the others clumsily called "Joe Banana," followed my teetotaler father home at midnight, after he closed shop. The noise would always awaken me. Just as well. I was expected to play a medley of Galway ditties on the piano. From the modest wooden house on the corner, the green one kitty-corner to Ben Cohen's variety store, came an incongruous chorus of toora-loora-looras. Whiskey-laced male voices, a blur of husky, off-key hums were led by a teenage soprano who had studied Bach études and Mozart rondos with Sister Jeanne Rosa, a French Catholic nun whom she adored.

Whatever superficial harmony had existed between my father and me at that time would soon disappear. It was May, 1950. I was seventeen years old, soon to graduate from Cambridge High and Latin School, a good student standing around waiting for my father's answer to a pathetic little speech I had made about wanting to go to college. My mother had made it clear I could do nothing without my father's blessing. That was a requirement, not a request. Without it, the tensions at home would be unbearable.

My father was in the final process of getting dressed to go to his office and he ignored me. First he tied his tie and buttoned down the collar of the Oxford blue shirt. Blue was his color, the classic blue of the Greek flag, a symbol of pride in his illustrious ancestry. Soundlessly he tied the laces of his perfectly polished black wing-tip Oxfords. It was as if I were not there. I wanted to leave but I seemed riveted to my place by some unknown force, frozen.

I knew instinctively what was coming. I was already aware of my father's Olympian view of women, his attitude of unconditional male superiority. I had never been allowed to have friends, to belong to school clubs, to go to parties or dances. My natural desire for peer sociability had already careened against his. He never used the word responsibility. It was my "duty" to help keep the house clean, to iron laundry, to do the dishes. This would get me carfare plus milk money. But one Valentine's Day he had given me two dollars and to this day I have his money and his card, a sentimental one signed, "Daddy." Now I was doing the unthinkable. I was asking for an education, something more forbidden than friendship.

When he finally put on his jacket and headed for the door, he turned around, looked at me as if I was crazy, and *laughed.* It was the classic laughter of men's mockery of women. That was his answer. Later I would tell my mother that I would not let him stop me.

Certain moments color everything you do. They are indelible. That confrontation with my father would mark everything in my life. If only my father had said I could try college for one term. That would have been enough of a beginning. But when he turned his back, when he walked away, I felt only hopelessness. I couldn't project beyond the pain. I was numbed by it.

This same confrontation had left me with a permanent insecurity. I became shy and introverted. I knew that my strength had to be absorbed from somewhere deep inside. I never thought it through in a logical way. I simply *felt* that success would be a part of my healing process, a way to show myself that I *could*. It was a crisis of self-worth. What I didn't know then was that my insecurity was the very thing motivating me. I needed to do something that would give me a sense of affirmation about myself. But, being scared, I imagined that someone, a rescuer, would have to *save* me from mediocrity. But who would it be? My mother, my ally, my most trusted friend, could not aid me materially. Although we were mutually helpless, my mother, a stoic to the end, did not *feel* helpless. My mother believed, truly, that if God is with you, no force on earth can stop you. Not even "daddy." She would say, over and over, in a gentle kind of brainwashing: "Something good comes from something bad." Oddly, the intensity of my ambition was sparked by my anger at the man who had laughed at me.

Ultimately I would go to Boston University, study journalism year-round at night for nearly seven years, while working days full-time. I'd pay my own way from wages earned in grubby government stockrooms and at metal file cabinets in the rear of government offices. My father didn't stop me. But he didn't help me either. It seemed to him that I was more or less an obedient daughter. By watching every penny, I even managed to pay a small room and board. Most weekday nights, at about ten P.M., he seemed unaware that I was walking upstairs, books in hand, going to my bedroom, while he watched television.

When I was twelve years old, my father gave me an illustrated version of *Little Women* by Louisa May Alcott. I treasured the book, reading it often. I felt an extraordinary kinship with the author. When my father had his heart attacks, it was I who took him to the emergency ward, except for the last time, when he died.

While I was going through his affairs, I discovered that he had been carrying a few of my first newspaper clippings neatly folded in his wallet. But he never mentioned my little victories, never praised me. I had always admired his devotion to hard work, his remarkable strength of purpose. It is his one characteristic I have emulated. Still I did not cry at his funeral. The bond between us had been severed when he laughed at my own ambition.

My father died penniless, in debt. I paid off the last of his monetary obligations. I would never feel the warmth of his smile to celebrate me. My father would always represent an unfulfilled void, a hunger that would gnaw when I least expected.

◇

THIRTY YEARS later I would meet Diana Nyad, famous long-distance swimmer, 1973 Phi Beta Kappa graduate of Lake Forest College. She was already an hour late for a scheduled New York interview. I was about to give up on her when by chance, I reached her on the telephone at home. She answered breathlessly. Nyad had just come from Cincinnati, completely forgetting the interview. But give her a few minutes, she'd pull herself together and come to talk. Another hour later, she did. I have never regretted waiting for her.

I had researched Nyad thoroughly before the interview. I knew she had a Greek father like me. But I had no right to assume that all Greek fathers were the same. As we talked, she zeroed in on her relationship with her father, whom she had not seen in years, a man who sent her messages through a third party once she became famous. She never answered the messages.

"I think I had an appallingly shallow relationship with my father. He was both ancient Greek and modern Greek. The ancient Greek spoke six languages and read me the *Odyssey.* He made me think." She continued breathlessly:

"The modern Greek was a fake, a con man. He could go to a party and have everyone eating out of his hand in five minutes. But he used his charm for false pretenses. When I was a kid, I called him a liar and a cheat in public and he gave me public belts with a hairbrush. I haven't seen him since I was thirteen or fourteen."

Nyad had a Greek father who beat her in public, a physical outrage. She succeeded in public, in sports, a *physical* arena, showing herself and the world she was stronger, tougher than the lashes her father inflicted. Nyad is the courageous marathon athlete who, in 1979, stroked eighty-nine miles from Bimini in the Bahamas to Jupiter, Florida. I asked if being a heroine were somehow tied up in showing her father up? The question made her squirm and blush. And eventually nod.

The story I wrote about Nyad was a subtle study in antipatriarchal motivation. My father tried to stop me from learning. It was a *silent* red light. I write in silence. Nyad's father tried to stop her in a physical way, with brute force. And she is a heroine in sports, a *physical* star. How well I understood Nyad's steady gaze of acquiescence.

Shackles come in the shape of a circle. So do crowns. I felt totally free of shackles many years later when, in an ironic twist, I found myself in the posh East Side Manhattan apartment of handsome, forty-four-year-old Prince Michael of Greece, a royal from my father's country.

The prince had married a commoner, forfeited his right to the throne and instead of playing among other European royals, had become a working author. The prince was a Greek blue-blood who happened to have a fictional

bestseller in Paris, *Sultana.* As we sat together, drinking
syrupy coffee from demitasse cups, the prince made the
observation that independence is not an easy mien, even
if your lineage is royal. The prince said people hate independence because it suggests you can't be controlled.

Unaware of my father's roots, the prince told me that
in 1970 he wrote a book, *History, My Sister.* In it he laid
bare his feelings about the hypocrisies of religion, history,
social life and even some members of his illustrious Greek
family.

"I was ostracized," he said, almost in a whisper. "This
went on for six months. I had the courage to put my truest
feelings to paper. But I was stunned by the negative reactions it brought. At first I thought to myself: 'What have
I done?' I doubted myself. I thought: 'Maybe they are right.
Maybe I am wrong.' Then I carefully reread everything I
had written. My words confirmed my ideas. I felt peaceful.
I knew I was right."

A prince of Greece was telling me that a sense of
"rightness" is what gives a dream staying power, what protects it from the permanent damage of criticism. Then he
said my eyes looked Mediterranean. It was a subtle way of
asking me my nationality. I told him my eyes were Greek.
Suddenly, out of the blue, Prince Michael asked about my
father. The tempo of our conversation had been so relaxed,
so frank, that almost despite myself, I told the prince about
my confrontation with my father. He confided that his wife,
an artist, also did not get her father's approval to be an
artist. The prince, the grandson of King George I of Greece
and the Grand Duchess Olga of Russia, suddenly stopped
clicking his worry beads. "How did *you* do it?" he asked.

I told the prince that what I believe substantiates courage, what fuels you, are the small successes that become
the beginning parts of the bigger quest, the ultimate success. The sum total of many little triumphs gain momentum
and add up significantly. I told him I see setbacks as temporary by letting go of the disabling idea that you are set

back forever. He made me feel he understood perfectly.

Maybe my father's natural chauvinism was understand-able. The women in his young life, clinging dependents, were beholden to him. It was during these conversational moments with the prince that I realized that I was finally able to verbalize my feelings about my father. I had over-come the deep resentments and could speak about them in a healthy way. My voice sounded wonderful to me. I had exorcised my own pain.

$$\diamond$$

IT WAS LATE October, 1975. Television newscasters blasted the arrival of the Anwar Sadats in Washington for a state visit, staying a few days at Blair House. What I wanted was a one-to-one interview with Jihan Sadat, an intimate look at a famous woman who used her femininity as a weapon, a woman who balanced a demanding marriage against her own independent self-vision.

Mrs. Sadat was only fifteen when she married this pow-erful and ambitious politician, a thirty-one-year-old di-vorced man who would one day be president of Egypt. Not only had the marriage flowered, so had she. A well-dressed English-Arab beauty, she would publicly speak out on birth control and ancient divorce laws in a Moslem country. She shook the culture and the tongues of powerful Egyptian men, who sarcastically dubbed her the "divine disturber of peace."

Mrs. Sadat was a member by marriage of the Egyptian hierarchy, the consort of President Sadat, who himself wasn't enthusiastic about women having a voice. She was the consummate politician making her way in a country that stifled women, a country made up of millions of men who still think the way my father thought. She was middle-aged and going to college, finally. She was out of her cage and trying to free other women from their black tents.

How was she doing what she was doing and simultaneously keeping a powerful husband, a world leader, happy and admiring? I wanted *her* to tell *me*.

Forget Mrs. Sadat, said my then-editor, saying it was a Washington story meant to be handled by Washington writers. What he wanted me to write instead was a wrap-up story of what items were selling in local department stores. I stood in front of his desk, on which his feet were propped, begging him to reconsider, telling him it would take only a day and he could dock me a day's vacation if I didn't produce.

A series of calls to the Egyptian embassy in Washington brought back a disappointing decision. Yes, Mrs. Sadat had been scheduled for interviews, but only with Barbara Walters and the *Washington Post*'s Sally Quinn.

When I argued that Boston should be included along with New York and Washington press, the ambassador himself, a Mr. Ghorbal from Harvard, sent me his own personal message. *If* I came to Washington on speculation, *if* I could get into Blair House and wait around indefinitely in an anteroom, *if* Mrs. Sadat decided to see me, "maybe" something could be arranged. I was also advised that Mrs. Sadat might not even be at Blair House during the proposed waiting period. "I'll take my chances," I thought, and went to Washington.

Secret Service agents intercepted me when I tried to cross the street in front of the Blair House main entrance. One agent reached into his breast pocket and pulled out a small card, advising me I was not on his "list." He meant I had not been cleared by the state department. I pulled out my press credentials, asking permission to get as far as the door. To my surprise, he nodded his head, yes. This got me into the anteroom the ambassador had mentioned. Several hours lapsed. I felt close to the interview, but far away.

Suddenly a stir of activity. The Sadats and entourage ceremoniously swept into Blair House, moving rapidly past the open door of the anteroom. In a split second, like a flash, Jihan Sadat passed my viewing range and we locked glances. Then the Sadats were gone. I heard a door close. It was quiet again.

But later I learned that Mrs. Sadat had asked who I was and Ambassador Ghorbal himself returned to tell me that Mrs. Sadat would see me privately, a forty-five-minute interview, which he called an "audience." The First Lady of Egypt found it interesting that a woman had come to see her on sheer chance. The Sadat story made the front page of the *Globe*'s Living section, November 2, 1975.

Mrs. Sadat, a doctor's daughter, revealed that her mother, an Englishwoman, objected strenuously to her marriage on many grounds but, "her disapproval was based on the fact that Anwar is not fair-skinned." It was a startling admission of racism within the ranks of Egypt's first family. The problem had long been settled, but not before a mother-in-law and son-in-law confronted each other as persons beyond color.

There are beautiful women everywhere who are contented to be adornments of powerful men. It is adulation by association, a background role. Mrs. Sadat seemed to be the rare female who turned her secondary position into a tool to establish her own personna, using her husband's power to personal advantage, all the while keeping the marriage intact. She seemed to be on a tightrope of self-adventure, balancing her role as wife of a Moslem world leader and suggesting certain age-old Moslem traditions be shattered.

In the interview, Mrs. Sadat told me she had gone on Egyptian radio "preaching" that Egypt's divorce laws be amended because "it's too utterly inhuman to the wife to live in such an environment of insecurity." According to Moslem doctrine, a man can divorce himself if he says three times: "I divorce thee." Then he goes to a sheik to make it official on paper. Later President Sadat had been asked on television how he reacted to his wife's crossing the line into his territory, politics. The president had replied with profound humor: "You cannot imagine how I shout."

The pivotal question was how this woman, a modernist, handled her man, an avowed traditionalist? Mrs. Sadat replied with a mixture of love and willingness to go along while actually shaking the boat.

"If I were to complain we don't have equal rights in our home because he is the head of the family, I wouldn't make any headway at all," she told me. "So I tell him of course he's the head of the family, and I always get my own way. Of course my husband is sometimes taken aback when he reads and hears things I've uttered. So he'll frown and say: 'Jihan, what's this all about?' I tell him what I've said is finished, so the words are best forgotten. Then he smiles."

"My marriage has succeeded because I taught myself the art of infinite patience. I learned early that my husband's life is a long, unending series of meetings. He wasn't home very much. I never picked a quarrel with him over the prolonged absences. Instead I took French lessons ..."

I wrote the story longhand on cheap paper in my hotel room, the story of a feminist who stretched herself and her ideas within the context of the Moslem religion. Mrs. Sadat had done this while remaining loved and loving. She had toughed it out in a subtle way, not with force, but with sweetness.

Mrs. Sadat had paralleled the same peaceful approach my mother insisted upon when I set upon my own little "revolution." My mother believed, as Mrs. Sadat believed, that a woman could quietly grasp opportunity, sometimes even manufacture her own chances, go *her* way without getting in *his* way. She never saw liberation as a public march, burning bras, carrying signs of protest. Liberation was a personal striving, a private war based on private resolution. My mother believed a woman's freedom was based on *adding* to whatever a woman has already achieved, not throwing everything out and beginning again. Whatever progress woman has made is too valuable to discard. It was a convincing let's-go-on-from-here attitude.

It is surprising, even frustrating, that very successful women don't always respect other very successful women. Feminists talk about the power of networking, of supporting one another and thus making the continuing path to success a smoother ride than men intended. But Gloria Steinem remains the only no-show interviewee in my career who offered no explanation, no apology, for not arriving at the Pierre Hotel in New York for a confirmed interview. Good Ol' Boy networking doesn't always work for females.

Another example I recall was Grace Jones, the black rock disco queen who had been the fabulous face on magazines like *Vogue* and *Harper's Bazaar*. Grace gave me a great interview for the *Boston Globe*. A few days after the story was published, "Entertainment Tonight," the syndicated television show, asked me to do a three-minute interview with her for national television at New York's Ritz-Carlton Hotel. The success of "Conversations" as a column seemed to be paying off and I felt certain the idea could be adapted for television. I had spent a lot of time in interviews, at first just listening hard, taking notes, memorizing quotes the moment they were uttered. Then I learned how to ask the right questions at the right time to get the best quotes. I had developed another "trick": unexpectedly rattling off facts gleaned from thorough research of the person interviewed—a birth date, names of family members, quotes from other stories. The celebrity was always surprised and flattered that I had come prepared, that I remembered things. This would become the connective tissue between questions, the glue that solidified a talk. At last, "Conversations" had become refined rather than rambling. I knew exactly what I wanted to ask Grace Jones on television, based on the successful print interview I had had with her a few weeks before.

Grace was indeed amazing. Lips slashed in fuchsia.

Head shaved except for a tuft of hair like a crown. She had an imperial gaze that began with a chin held high and ended with magnetic eyes that were touched with arrogance. Then, of course, there was her biography. She had a baby by Jean-Paul Goude, a former art director of *Esquire* magazine. They were not married, which seemed to open the whole subject of fathering. Besides, there were tantalizing paternal credentials. Her father, a strict Pentecostal minister, Robert Winston Jones, had not allowed her to watch television or listen to the radio, an attempt to protect his beautiful daughter from being corrupted by commercialism. What did he think of her now? I fantasized that when I asked that question, the camera would zoom in for an extreme close-up. Grace Jones's face was outrageous and noble at the same time. While the camera held steady on that contradiction, I would ask if she and her father communicated with each other. In my *Globe* interview, she had told me that what was wrong between her and her father was noncommunication. When she realized she had confided more than she intended, she moved to cover it up. She also hastily assured me that the breach was healed. "And now we communicate," she said, "because he reached the point at which he respects the fact that I left home and made something of my life. He's been to my house. He likes the way I live: neat, clean, orderly. I'm more like him than either of us ever realized. We both like simplicity, uncomplicated situations. He is an independent who respects my independence, but"—and here she hesitated, as if her voice were going to break—"my father has never seen me perform."

Jones had made it sound as if she were on good terms with her father. He was welcoming back his prodigal daughter who, in fact, had a loyal homosexual audience. But I knew the truth of the real father-daughter relationship slipped when she admitted that he had never seen her on a nightclub stage with her whips and chains. Maybe he couldn't face the reality of a rebel child in public performance.

Maybe he was shocked. In the *Globe* interview she had
articulated one of her dreams: "It's having my father's approval of my work," she had said. I was going to bring that
up in the television interview. I felt that the print interview
was a warm-up for the screen. I also felt safe in putting
such questions to Jones because I had witnesses and doc-
umentation, the "Entertainment Tonight" field team and
the tape itself.

There's a big difference between newspaper interviews and television interviews. Celebrities are *nice* on
television because it's like being onstage, with camera-lights-
action. Newspaper interviews aren't as disciplined. They
tend to be sloppier. The big challenge is, of course, to keep
the person you're interviewing on track. Print interviews
wander easily. Television is rigid with everyone working
hard to appear relaxed. Print interviews *are* more relaxed
because there's no audience. And, not incidentally, a print
interview allows the celebrity the chance to deny quotes,
especially if there's no tape recorder. On television, everything is on the record, literally.

The day of the television interview finally came. The
crew and I were set up, ready to roll, but where was Grace
Jones? We waited and waited and waited. Several frantic
telephone calls to her agent offered no reassurance. No
one knew exactly where she was or when she'd materialize.
At first the crew was bored. Then they became suspicious
about the efficiency of my arrangements. *They* were there.
Where the hell was *she?* What prevented them from walking out was the fact that they were getting paid overtime.
But I was a beginner, and I wasn't producing Grace Jones.
I stood around in my hotel room as frozen as the day I
faced my father to ask to go to college. The room was
jammed with equipment. The lights were ready to burst.
Nearly two hours later, Jones calmly strolled in, a large
bottle of chilled champagne in hand for everybody. Charming, she was. Gregarious, she was. Trailing behind her were
an agent with a Cheshire Cat smile and a young black man

who looked like Michael Jackson. She described this man as her cosmetician. Indeed, he flicked pink powder on her nose just before the cameras whirred into action. I tried to conduct the interview as planned, asking the difficult questions about Jones's father, but I was totally unnerved by her lateness and lack of respect for our time. The camera picked up the tension, even magnified it. The interview had nowhere near the impact I knew it could have had. The Grace Jones tape was never used on "Entertainment Tonight."

There have been other memorable incidents where networking was unheard of, a foreign language. Maria Burton, adopted daughter of Elizabeth Taylor and Richard Burton, agreed to an interview. I was told to meet Burton, a German by birth, in the Manhattan office of her agent. I did. Only the way the interview was set up, I had to step down, into a scooped-out area like a little pit, and Burton sat higher up, on what seemed like a platform, and looked down at me. The person who arranged this interview was a female publicist who sat behind the barrier of her desk, near Burton, absorbing the interview with a blank expression. The physical inequality, one high and one low, seemed like a form of intimidation. Burton was evasive, faintly riled. She chain-smoked throughout the interview. To say I was uncomfortable is gross understatement. I had read a lot of stories, fables perhaps, about her growing up with Liz and Dick as mommy and daddy and I asked questions that I thought, I *hoped*, might get the conversation started. "Did you really roughhouse it with Liz when you were a child?" "Yes." "Are you still close to your father?" "Yes." We *really* were on different levels, Maria Burton and I.

Mama Jolie Gabor, who turned out to be a wonderful interview once she settled down, had a loud tantrum in the main lobby of New York's Plaza Hotel, just outside the Palm Court. She was complaining bitterly, and quickly gathered a fascinated audience, about the fact that I had not sent a prepaid limousine to transport her a few blocks from her apartment to my hotel where we had planned to meet. It was raining hard. I had come from Boston. She had come a few blocks. I let her have her tantrum and, when she was through, invited her to sit down with me and have coffee. When I calmed her down she talked openly about Eva and Zsa Zsa and Magda.

People think sweetness and kindness are the same as stupidity, as being a hick. It took a long time for me to prove that niceness, if it's sincere, pays off. But for a long time I thought the only way to get good quotes was to be a hard hitter. It took me time to learn how to swallow my pride, put my personal feelings aside, my vulnerability, without losing my sensitivity.

Women don't always show other women journalists a sense of mutuality. I say that knowing that I myself have often refused to give other journalists, both men and women, private telephone numbers of celebrities or their home addresses. I don't readily share story contacts or story ideas or private information. There is too much rivalry for stories and I have established a hard-earned reputation for exclusivity. The mutuality that I'm talking about is respect, plain old-fashioned good manners. That's what gives a journalist style and elegance. It's something I'm always seeking in the people I interview. There have been times when it has been very hard to find.

$$\Diamond$$

IN MAY, 1983, I was assigned to interview Nora Ephron, author of the bestselling book *Heartburn,* a thinly veiled autobiographical account of a pregnant woman who discovers her husband is having an affair. Ephron's second husband, Watergate reporter Carl Bernstein, reportedly had an affair with Mrs. Peter Jay, wife of the former British ambassador and daughter of James Callaghan, Britain's ex-prime minister.

We met for tea at New York's Ritz-Carlton hotel. Ephron is a flamboyantly famous journalist and she was feeling her mettle. As we sat down to begin the interview Ephron whipped out a question that was meant to imply her superiority. "Do you take shorthand?" Ephron asked, arching her brows till they were half-hidden under her long bangs. She assumed the mantle of an executive about to embark on serious dictation.

Nora Ephron is a 1962 Wellesley College graduate, a product of Beverly Hills, daughter of famous Hollywood screenwriters Phoebe and Henry Ephron. She is also a witty author whose work has appeared in *Esquire* and *Newsweek.* Now Ephron, a journalist whose analyst helped her come to grips with marital woes, was treating me, another journalist, as if I were nothing more than a note-taking machine.

During the interview, Ephron waved her wrist and demanded that the grammar be corrected in a quote I, in fact, rejected as too inconsequential to record. The quote Ephron referred to was about her "privileged background." My idealistic approach to the one-to-one interview was being shot to hell. Yet I wanted to preserve the "oneness" I so valued. That was more important than allowing hurt feelings to linger. I had to concentrate on the quality of the interview itself, something that was not very easy.

What Ephron didn't know was that I had actually scribbled in my notebook, but didn't use in the story, this impression: "N.E. can be catty. Claw competition is classic in the female cat." Meanwhile, I asked Ephron if her book wasn't the ultimate revenge against Bernstein, the usually successful ploy of having the last laugh in public?

"Revenge?" Ephron replied, eyes widening. "I'd be Pollyannaish to say it didn't cross my mind." That's the quote I used in the prologue of the story.

Journalism is a work that carries with it certain unspoken ethics. Knowing what's right and what's wrong is not enough because there are more grays than black-and-whites, more imponderables. You have to envision your role in a clear-cut way, playing fair when circumstances aren't. You have to be involved and uninvolved at the same time.

The pen is indeed mightier than the sword. It was a great temptation to use the Ephron story as retaliatory ammunition. Occasionally I have succumbed to that weakness. It has brought me no satisfaction. Getting to the truth of that person is the greatest power. It means you have disarmed the person, reduced the defenses. Instead of waging a war of words, you establish dialogue. The interview becomes a kind of informal high level diplomacy.

Ephron caught my bait: "The last thing I wanted people to think was that I was squashed flat, wallowing in self-pity, defenseless, powerless, vulnerable in a hopelessly wounded way. To give up that feeling is a major move," Ephron told me. "You have to accept responsibility for your own life. You have to stop blaming whomever you're blaming. But there's a kind of freedom in deciding to do what you have to do."

This woman had turned her life around, laughing at herself in public, making a big, clever joke about an erring ex-husband. By so doing, she had cleverly added new celebrity to her career, reconstructed herself and her life. I wrote a story about her courage.

◇

GOING AGAINST the odds is painful. But it's good exercise for a journalist because it forces you inward, making you tap your own resources. Writing is work you do totally alone, a solitary craft by which you convey the energy of the spoken word onto an empty page.

When I was in my twenties, I scribbled three five-hundred-word pieces of fiction and the *Boston Post* bought all three for five dollars apiece. Once I had written a story about the work of a watercolor artist and sent it to a local paper to use for free. They did, word for word, under someone else's by-line.

Today I am selfish about interviews. I do not want to lose them. Opportunities present themselves once, and that's it. You can't tell the person you're interviewing: "I'll come around another time, when you're in a better mood." You have to cope with the mood and the environment, or lose the story.

When I told my mother I would not be stopped, I didn't know that would mean not letting the person I was *interviewing* stop me. A two-way tantrum would be an automatic forfeit of the interview. *That's* what made me control my temper when confronting difficult people. When I felt the urge to stomp off I forced myself to act as if I were a detached observer watching my own encounter from a distance, which is how I turned several potentially bad interviews into good ones.

$$\Diamond$$

BILL MOYERS, CBS-TV's extraordinary commentator, showed me the door of his office even before I began the actual interview. It was June, 1983, and I had come to interview him in New York. He recoiled when I explained my story approach. Personalization was not something that interested him. Without changing his pleasant facial expression, he moved from behind his desk and led me by the elbow to the door, suggesting that I interview his colleague, Charles Kurault, whose office was just down the hall.

I stood at the door, facing the powerful ex-publisher of the Long Island newspaper, *Newsday,* now a $1-million-a-year network television commentator. I knew two things about Moyers. He was a ministerial man. He had taught Christian ethics at Baylor University after receiving a Bachelor of Divinity degree in 1959 from Southwestern Baptist

Theological Seminary. He had also been press secretary to the late President Johnson, a man who had conquered Washington as an unflappable, self-assured White House official. He was not a man who would bend easily.

I made a split second decision to gamble on his sense of fair play.

He had his hand on the doorknob, as if to turn it. I asked him to please give me a chance at the interview. If he didn't like the way it was going, I'd leave of my own volition. He looked hard at me. He looked *through* me. Without changing his expression, he walked back to his desk. I followed him, though uninvited. He used his desk as a barrier and he took out a cigar. As he lit it, as he puffed, Moyers told me that cigar smoking was merely a ploy, a trusty prop. This simple admission of vulnerability opened up what became a very successful interview.

"When I was at the White House," he said, "reporters would zero in with questions that would bring LBJ's wrath on my head. There were a lot of stakes with every answer. The few seconds I bought lighting a cigar or taking a puff were, for me, great moments of composure. Watch cigar smokers: they appear calm with a few exceptions, like Archie Bunker. Behind the appearance is a restless, seething current. I confess to that."

Moyers admitted to great sensitivity and insatiable curiosity, and I told him those were two basic requirements of a good journalist. Talking like a colleague, he likened fine journalism to the art of bringing "real people to real people." We delved into the characteristics of journalists, how they are drawn to the eccentricities of human behavior and imagination, how they love to go to new places and talk new ideas to new people. Moyers was, of course, talking about himself and I took it all down. He commented wryly that there are people who say Christopher Columbus didn't know where he was going or where he'd been and he didn't do it with his own money. "Journalism is a lot like that," Moyers said, smiling. "Journalism is like walking down Broadway, with a different play at every door. It's intoxicating. Dangerous, too. You tend to be a voyeur, not a participant."

I smiled to myself. I had gotten the story by *not* being a voyeur, but an insistent participant to the man who would have rather been left alone.

$$\Diamond$$

IT IS ONE thing to face polite ejection, like Moyers's. It is quite another to face outrageousness, to decide what kind of bad behavior is worth bearing to get a story.

Details of Mickey Rooney's personal history, culled from his clip file, produced a string of dramas. Married eight times. Eight children. Heavy alimony burdens. Made an estimated $12 million fortune. Declared bankruptcy in 1962. Twenty years later, at age sixty-one, critics were raving about a Rooney renaissance. He was starring in the hit Broadway musical *Sugar Babies,* making $20,000 a week and a healthy profit percentage. Rooney, a born-again Christian, was also a born-again star.

Rooney, a short, balding man of glaring contradictions, hates publicity, a fact I didn't know before the interview. He introduced himself to me, not by name, but as a "public private person." Our encounter was a study in offstage theatrics. Rooney was twenty minutes late for a rare promised forty-five-minute conversation. Minutes before the two o'clock matinee, the paunchy actor unabashedly stripped down to his undershorts, loose unironed white boxers. No warning. No apology. But suddenly out of nowhere a gay male dresser materialized and began helping Rooney into ridiculous red long johns. Rooney looked like a helpless child getting ready for bed, being dressed in one-piece, snap-front pajamas. Only this was star treatment.

My interview questions were unacknowledged, drowned by Rooney's voice, which needed no microphone. Rooney delivered a loud, discombobulated soliloquy about Fourth of July patriotism. He bellowed, claiming he had to be heard over the mild hum of the dressing room air conditioner. Then he said something strange, something I did not understand. "Man's only power is regretting having attained it." What did he mean? When I asked, Rooney got mean.

"Take it down. Print it. There will be intelligent people out there who'll understand," he ordered. I was stung but I don't think he even noticed. I repeated the question. This time, Rooney lowered his voice several decibels, put a calloused palm on the hand taking notes and quoted the Bible with surprising fervor. Clearly he was an actor *acting:* "What good is a man who has gained the world and lost his soul?" he asked in sermonlike tones. Then he put on a battered top hat, an oversized tweed coat, and asked me if that statement was too difficult for me to understand. His tone was simultaneously sarcastic and sweet.

In the distance, the orchestra was in full swing and a microphoned voice was ordering the cast to the wings. Rooney shot out of the dressing room in the bowels of Boston's Wang Center for the Performing Arts, insisting that I wait for his return. But I had the story, the "other" side of a great personality, a talented man whose intensity could sting, an original who had dared to thumb his nose at me, a press person, and almost remain a gentleman.

$$\Diamond$$

THE LATE Robert Frost said it first. Sylvester Stallone, a man who beat the odds to a pulp, quoted it to me in the backseat of a chauffered gray Cadillac limousine: "We will dance around the ring and suppose, but the answer sits in the middle and knows." Stallone said it quietly, slowly, enunciating every word, hoping the impact would sink in. We had just met and he was quoting poetry to me. There is no callousness about Sylvester Stallone, only luxury and elegance. His handshake has the texture of fine silk and he smells wonderful, "Gucci," perhaps, and we are gliding to our luncheon destination from an East Side hotel to the Russian Tea Room, a few blocks away, a distance easily walked. Stallone's fingernails are manicured and he is carrying new black leather gloves, absentmindedly hitting them against his left hand like a miniature whip. There is a rakishness about this thirty-five-year-old millionaire. But the cockiness is softened because he is talking sentimentally about "dreams," about removing himself from a juvenile delinquent from Hell's Kitchen with a troublemaker's record, to where he is now, a superstar. He is describing his father as "violent" and his mother as "eccentric." Stallone wrote *Rocky* and in the backseat of that car he describes himself as the prototypical Rocky, a nowhere fighter who beats his opponent, beats the odds, to become a champion. Stallone lives in a million-dollar Pacific Palisades home that has adorned the pages of *Architectural Digest,* but he is still happy to eat out of the pot on the stove rather than on a plate, a nouveau millionaire who dares to be himself. I tell him that is the height of confidence, being yourself, and he laughs. I want to know *why* he is laughing. First he talks numbers. Hollywood producers offered him $360,000 for the original script for *Rocky* and wanted Burt Reynolds to play Rocky. Stallone held out, selling *Rocky* for $75,000, and the promise to star in it. By the time we were having this lunch, in April, 1982, *Rocky* had been nominated for ten Academy Awards and won for Best Picture. I coax Stallone to tell me where he got his *nerve.* Is it manufactured? Is it in his genes? All phony, he says, a put-on, pseudo, make believe. What in hell are you talking about? I ask. And he delivers the ultimate soliloquy about going against the odds and winning.

"I manufactured my self-confidence. I lied to myself. When I was fired as a mugger in Woody Allen's *Bananas,* that almost killed my confidence. It was a silent bit. But, up to then, the most important role I ever played. He [Woody Allen] said my friend and me, we didn't look intimidating enough. I was crushed. But this kid with me, he was short, he had tremendous confidence. And he's saying: 'C'mon, let's go back. Let's put Vaseline and mud on our faces and look that guy straight in the eye, act tough, and get our jobs back.' And I'm saying, 'Hey, forget it.' And he's dragging me back. Okay, so he does the talking. I don't say a word, and . . . *and we get our jobs back.*

"Now I'll never take no for an answer. I told myself, if this kid can do it, no reason why I can't do it. Everyone has insecurities. Our confidence is an artificial state. It needs to be reinforced. Confidence stays strong only when the decisions you make are right. When your decisions are wrong, you can lose your confidence. But you have to kid yourself along, fake it.

"Boxing is the one sport where a man is stripped bare of charades, put against another man who wants what he wants, the prize. But there's only one prize. The humiliation factor of losing is enormous. There are the hot lights, the audience a few feet away. And what's worse than being beaten physically, dropping to the canvas, a man with his arms raised in triumph standing over you?

"The greatest fear I have in life is fear of failure. The person I fear most is me. I always remind myself of my defeats. If I'm tired, I say, 'Oh, the hell with it! Give it up!' Self-loathing sets in and it can be destructive. But I face myself squarely and say: 'You realize you didn't put out one hundred percent?' And that's good. Self-loathing makes me do better.

"The thought that I could be Rocky was blind, blind belief in myself. Many people said I couldn't do it. When people tell you the dream is impossible, you have to turn your ears off and turn your eyes inward. I told myself continuously: 'I will do it.' I pretended ignorance when people criticized me. Rather than debate, I said: 'You're right, I'm too short to play Rocky.' But I knew in my heart that I could. One person said, 'You're stupid, you can't play a part you've written.' I agreed. What I was doing was short-circuiting my detractors. I knew, in my heart, what I could become.

"I really had this fear of unrealized dreams. Every dream I ever had never came true. When I was in the third grade, I had a fantasy. I thought I was Superboy. I wore red leotards and red shorts under my school clothes and a barber's cape from my father's shop. I painted S on my sweatshirt. I was an emaciated kid. I had skinny legs. My friend Jimmy, I showed him my costume in the men's room—told him I was Superboy. So he told the teacher, and the teacher made me strip in front of the whole class. And there I was in my Superboy clothes, everyone laughing. It was cruel. It was the end of my fantasies until I saw Hercules in the movies. Then I wanted to be Hercules. Hercules was ethical and physical, a strong father figure. That's what I wanted to be as a man.

"I had Superboy and Hercules and eventually I envisioned Rocky. I created a character that was basically me, the way I wish I was. When they offered me the money for the script, I had this fear of not seeing me to the end. It would have been embittering to see someone take it away. It seemed like death to me. I walked away from the offers. I'd rather have the script in my possession and the dream unrealized than give it up."

THIS SIDE
OF LOVE

THE HIGHLY improbable was happening. Superstar Liz Taylor, six-times married Hollywood beauty who was still wearing Richard Burton's legendary 69.42 carat Cartier diamond ring, and I were rivals vying for the attention of Iranian Ambassador Ardeshir Zahedi, former son-in-law of the shah.

Liz, who had a highly publicized 1976 two-week romance with Zahedi at the Iranian embassy in Washington, D.C., where I had also stayed at Zahedi's invitation, wanted to marry Zahedi. It was rumored that the shah, whose daughter Princess Shanaz had once been married to Zahedi, forbade it. Within a few months, Liz married Senator John Warner and conquered a new audience, Washington, citadel of concentrated political power. Washington was a stage unlike Hollywood, unlike Broadway, and Liz was a star in this new arena until she and Warner were divorced. Meanwhile Zahedi, who once told me privately, "There is nothing I ever wanted to do I have not done," was being quoted in gossip columns as saying Liz was "fat."

Certainly I had an affection for Zahedi, but I was never in love with him. Even now the sentimental bond continues. Zahedi invited me to several impressive embassy parties, private ones not covered by the press, and I admired

his blend of sophistication and earthiness, opposite qualities that blurred into a unique charm. Zahedi now lives in
Switzerland, is reportedly near the top of the Ayatollah
Khomeini's hit list, is constantly surrounded by a battery
of bodyguards, and has on his head a reward purported to
be $1 million. This is the same man who sometimes writes
me that his mother is ailing and his daughter, Princess
Mahnaz, is blooming. Despite the time and distance between us, he tells me, in his own handwriting, that he
"respects" and "admires" me. He always signs his letters
with "love."

Several years ago, I moved to a new townhouse in
Boston and one of the first times I answered the doorbell,
I discovered a delivery man holding a huge bouquet of
exotic flowers as carefully as if he were holding a newborn
baby. The lovely flowers were not in the usual box or
arranged in a vase. They were tied together with big red
silk streamers and were meant to go from the absent arms
of Zahedi, who had sent them, to mine.

The ambassador, a natural romantic, could always make
the most ordinary gestures seem extraordinary. He always
personalized things. He could never be accused of being
remote. A loving note accompanied the bouquet and I have
kept it with the many, many cards that came with the huge
vases of long-stemmed American Beauty roses, two or three
dozen at a time, which Zahedi sent frequently, even when
the newspapers carried stories about his togetherness with
Liz.

My relationship with Zahedi started when I was sent
in December, 1974, to the Iranian embassy to interview
him for a special *Globe* profile. It was a luncheon meeting,
the ambassador and me alone at his formal dining table,
being served courses by a uniformed English butler wearing white gloves. The ambassador seemed pleasantly surprised that a woman journalist was asking what he called
"intelligent" questions. Zahedi, by then known as a "playboy diplomat," was amused that I took copious notes while
pretending to eat.

The interview quickly became personal, as if Zahedi wanted me to know him as a man rather than merely the most sought-after bachelor in Washington since Henry Kissinger. There was no mistaking a physical chemistry between us. Zahedi was introducing himself to me, not casually, but with sweeping Technicolor details of his attitude and style, as if reaching out to me. Zahedi spoke about friendship and love as if they were just ahead of us. What he said reflected Oriental wisdom of many centuries, but he gave the comments the stamp of his individuality.

"When you travel with someone who has strong ideas of where to go, what to do, and they are opposed to yours," he said, "the question of compromise comes up. Without a degree of mutual surrender of the wills of each person, a friendship cannot survive because it cannot stand the rigors of time." Zahedi told me that if you ask a friend for money and that person hesitates, even for a fraction of a second, he is not your friend.

"And," he continued, "if you gamble with a friend and he is a bad loser, he will be a fair weather friend. The way in which a man accepts his own losses is a symbol of how he'll treat yours."

I had seen a picture of his ex-wife, Princess Shanaz, in a Paris scandal sheet, a pretty woman with a fine figure wearing a teeny-weeny bikini, stretched in the sun like a lazy cat. She had, by then, married an Iranian businessman and was living splendidly in the south of France. Zahedi took the blame for the separation and the divorce. "It's very traumatic," he said, "to discover that you're married to a woman with whom you simply cannot get along. Unfortunately, there's no acceptable way to forecast the difficulties." The Moslem religion does not sanction premarital relationships.

I asked him what kind of women fascinated him *now.* Zahedi blurted that beautiful women made him "passionate." At that moment, I absentmindedly reached for the wrong fork, something which Zahedi's English butler corrected by subtly handing me the right one. Zahedi, sitting

at his elaborate table with the large silver peacock cen-
terpiece, pretended not to notice my *faux pas* and the fact
that my hand trembled as I scribbled notes. "After you look
at a pretty face for five minutes," he continued, "boredom
sets in. Truly beautiful women have a scintillating spirit,
an alive mind and an intelligent approach to the business
of living. Glamor is lost if the charm doesn't emanate from
the inside out." I thought to myself: Zahedi would probably
be the perfect lover, expert and painstakingly caring. But
he's a man who's looking for the perfect woman.

I tried to turn the intense conversation from love to
friendship. How? Zahedi announced that he *never* invited
real friends to embassy parties covered by *Vogue* and *Wom-
en's Wear Daily.* Those parties were, he said, "business"
oriented. Only his "real" friends were invited to private
gatherings. I asked his definition of friendship. "The friend
who's a friend comes to you voluntarily when you're tasting
life's bitterness, when the sting makes you feel terribly
alone," he said. These are the prophetic words he uttered
when he reigned over Washington like a social god, five
years before the Ayatollah Khomeini took over Iran on
February 12, 1979, and he found his friends were few.

◇

AFTER MY interview with Zahedi appeared in the *Globe,* I
never expected to see or hear from the ambassador again.
But then the roses started coming. Lots of them. Later,
Zahedi invited my mother to a private embassy dinner. He
sent her caviar the next day and a note that she never let
me read. A bond developed between them immediately.
Years later, when she was dying, Zahedi sent her many
baskets of fine delicacies to the hospital, unaware that she
couldn't eat. Zahedi even asked my permission to speak to
her by telephone from the embassy and seemed genuinely
saddened to hear she could no longer speak. When she

died, he called me and later wrote me a beautiful letter which I still have, a letter urging me to continue in the beauty and spirit he admired in my mother.

Ambassador Ardeshir Zahedi was one of the few interviews I've done where, in my quest for mutuality, I stepped beyond the line of professionalism and reached out to him as a friend. I have never regretted breaking my own rule of distancing because he opened to me his door, and the doors to valuable, even historic interviews.

It was Zahedi who gave an elegant Sunday night embassy reception to honor my sister, a doctor, who was then in Washington to address the Senate on her work with closed-circuit television medicine in Alaska. My mother came to that party. She and Zahedi were inseparable that evening. He personally escorted her to dinner. He seated her to his right and concentrated on her, treating me as "second best," relying on the Moslem concept of mother-courtship as a statement of honorable intentions.

Zahedi is a true Moslem. You could never call him a feminist. But it was he who personally arranged an interview with the otherwise-inaccessible Empress Farah Diba, the shah's Paris-educated wife. During the shah's state visits Washington's Blair House, where the royal family sometimes stayed, was always surrounded by hordes of television and newspaper journalists who waited for hours to snag the shah and his wife for a brief "statement." I swept past them all, past the suspicious Secret Service, past Iranians begging to see their leader, past two jewelry vendors asking to put their sparklers on a table the empress would pass to get to this interview, mine. Zahedi had arranged an exclusive one-to-one interview with the empress, a story aggressively sought after by the international press.

In Iran, Zahedi had me driven by Mercedes, with a translator, to the massive Tehran palace of the empress's mother, Madame Farideh Diba, widow of an army captain. We were nearly forced off the twisted road by a man in a jeep. At the time I thought it was a near-miss accident.

Now I wonder if an enemy of the shah was already flexing his muscles around those associated or involved with the royal family. Madame Diba talked openly to me about her ambitions for her daughter, how she encouraged the empress to study architecture, a man's profession, at a time when Iranian women still disguised themselves in black robes. It was an inside story being done inside the family palace.

As a journalist, I wondered whether or not Ambassador Zahedi, with his worldwide connections, was using our friendship to gain publicity for Iran's royal family. The truth was that the royal family was getting more publicity than it wanted or needed. Every major network and wire service and newspaper was after what I was getting. Zahedi happened to be in the powerful position of picking and choosing interviews and he made me one of the chosen.

Zahedi neither criticized nor praised my stories. He was neutral, noncommittal, about what I wrote. And I wrote exactly what I saw and felt. He gave me such a free hand, interviews without conditions, that a group of female Iranian journalists traveling with the shah once asked me if they could sit in on my interview with the empress at Blair House. Immediately I saw the danger of losing the exclusivity and impact of my story. I would be conducting an interview witnessed by other journalists taking notes for stories that would appear under their by-line.

Thievery is as natural as breathing in newspapering. I said no, emphatically. The spokesperson making the request countered that Barbara Walters had allowed the group access to her network interview. I told the person, a glamorous brunette, that the Barbara Walters interview was filmed for immediate release, that the public would be seeing it within a day. Barbara Walters could not be beaten in terms of interview content or timing and she could afford to cooperate. I could not. Whatever quotes the Iranians used would have to be credited to Barbara Walters. That obviously was not the case for me. The woman walked away in a huff.

When the shah was dying, when Khomeini took the American hostages and stunned the world with his mad arrogance, when President Jimmy Carter seemed helpless and cut off from Iran, the shah's twin sister, Princess Ashraf Pahlavi, escaped to her New York townhouse. From his Switzerland hideaway, Zahedi arranged for me to interview Princess Ashraf, who had once survived a point-blank assassination attempt. Princess Ashraf talked openly to me, spilling gut feelings about the downfall of her family and her country, the impending death of her brother, her concept of destiny.

It was a remarkable interview, done in the presence of two armed bodyguards wearing fine English tailored business suits. Zahedi made it possible for me to get these several major stories. But Zahedi also showed me that friendship with a journalist is fickle. So was his romance with Liz Taylor.

$$\Diamond$$

IT WAS THE early summer of 1976 and Zahedi, master showman, had arranged a spectacular trip to Iran, inviting a cross-section of international socialites. Chicago's Mrs. John Swearingen, and Washington's Mr. and Mrs. Page Hufty, who had oil connections, were there, as well as movie stars like Cloris Leachman and Connie Stevens. I, too, was invited. I found myself in the company of Francesca Hilton, Zsa Zsa's daughter and Mary Jameson, Eva Gabor's stepdaughter.

Liz Taylor was to be the ambassador's star-in-residence on the trip, his publicity-drawing card. Zahedi didn't go to Iran but he came to Kennedy Airport to bid his hand-picked guests a fond farewell in front of the press. He and Liz were posed as a couple. Still cameras clicked. Television cameras whirred. The couple stood together holding hands in the spotlight. The scene was a perfect example of the ironies of star-crossed love. Connie Stevens, who had once been married to Eddie Fisher, one of Liz's ex-husbands, stood next to me on the sidelines. We were both watching Zahedi watching Liz.

Zahedi had a cousin, Firouz Zahedi, a handsome young man with more than his share of *savoir-faire*, who was to look after Liz's every need. A case of J&B scotch was delivered to her on the plane where she had a private compartment. Liz Taylor traveled with a maid, a hairdresser, and a makeup artist. During the long flight from New York to Tehran, Liz stunned the ambassador's guests by appearing in a lounge wearing hair rollers, a muu-muu, and makeup over her makeup. And later, at Persepolis, where Zahedi had arranged a fantastic nighttime tour of the specially lit ancient ruins, Liz Taylor's hotel room and mine turned out to be the same. After much confusion, she got it and I had to move.

The ambassador had asked me to keep the interview with the empress's mother secret, not to print it until I returned to Boston. No other writer on the trip had been invited to the family palace. The ambassador wanted it kept quiet until his guests returned to the United States, until it would be an interview impossible to duplicate.

The interview was conducted in the ballroom-size sitting room of the empress's mother, a big rectangular room with a glass wall overlooking a sparkling turquoise pool in which the shah's children cavorted joyfully. A massive manicured tropical garden surrounded the pool, which was punctuated with big, old, twisted olive trees. I saw bodyguards crouched in the foliage, men carrying rifles, the Iranian equivalent of the Secret Service. They seemed to tense when the leaves rustled. The shah's men looked like thugs who could get trigger-happy.

That evening, still exhilarated over getting an exclusive story, I learned that Liz Taylor was being entertained at Zahedi's private home at a party hosted by his then-teenage daughter. I was not invited. I have always felt that Liz was angry about our run-in at the Persepolis hotel, that somehow we were both assigned to the best room. She certainly knew my name. Maybe she insisted that Zahedi exclude me. Later I made subtle inquiries about Zahedi's party and an Embassy spokesman told me I certainly was on Zahedi's "number one list" and that the invitation somehow got "lost."

But the shah, Zahedi's boss and ex-father-in-law, had made his opinion clear about Liz Taylor at an earlier palace reception. There was to be an outdoor rendezvous on the grounds of the main royal palace in Tehran. All of Zahedi's guests were summoned there to meet the empress, the shah's social emissary. It was early afternoon. Liz arrived by private limousine wearing a black cocktail dress and thick necklace studded with chunky diamonds. Everyone else, even the Chicago and Texas oil millionaires, came on buses.

Surprisingly, Liz was not escorted inside the cool of the palace, but had to stand out in the sunny palace garden and wait, just like everyone else. Finally it was announced that the empress would be arriving in a moment. A receiving line was formed. Liz went to the head of the line, near a big sliding glass door she had been advised the empress would use.

Perhaps the empress saw Liz. Perhaps the empress was acting on the shah's orders. I don't know exactly what happened. But somehow I, who had stood last in line, became the first person the empress greeted. She emerged suddenly out of the door nearest me and lingered in conversation, reminiscing pleasantly about our Blair House interview. The empress and I spoke as if we were sorority sisters happy to be meeting again. Liz Taylor was the last guest to be greeted and the empress's handshake was brief, the reception to her cool. Liz Taylor obviously was not a star on the shah's stage. Rumor was that Zahedi was ordered by his boss, the shah, to discontinue the Liz liaison. Apparently he did and Liz and Senator Warner became a duo.

Late one autumn evening months before this trip Za-

hedi and I sat alone in front of a roaring fireplace in the
dark of his private quarters, drinking brandy from giant
snifters, his arms encircling me. Zahedi had a mesmerizing
magic about his kisses, total assurance in his ability to
please a woman. He was almost my big romance. But next
day, just before I left his residence, his chauffeured navy
blue Mercedes waiting for me, I knew I would not be
coming back. Telltale signs of his many lovers had surfaced
and I was disenchanted.

The maid advised me curtly that the ranch mink coat
in his downstairs closet was for the temporary use of "any"
woman for the duration she was in the ambassador's company. And in my private bath, I discovered a half-used bottle
of Jean Patou's "Joy" perfume, not a fresh bottle especially
for me. Love's little details were askew and the sentiment
between us became simple camaraderie.

$$\Diamond$$

I HAVE ALWAYS loved love, that great and mysterious human
connection. Love brings two spirits together as friends, or
two lovers into physical oneness. There are a million var-
iations between the two contrasts of platonic and sexual
love. When I discover these myriad subtle shadings, usually
by pure chance in intense interviews, I cannot be impas-
sive. Love is one of the true treasures of a person and I
react to it reverently because there is a purity to it, a giving.
Maybe my respect for love stems from the void I feel about
never having experienced the precious love of lasting romance. But, once or twice in my life, I have had quick glimpses
of love before it disappeared from my horizon. The memories still hold me in their grasp. And I still hold on to the
old feeling that if true love has touched other people, maybe
it will find me too.

Ray Bolger, the scarecrow in the film classic, *The Wizard of Oz,* gave me this definition of love over bloody

marys: "You can have Freud and Schopenhauer. I'll take Oz. The Oz story has two different messages: all a person needs to get through life is his heart, his courage and his brain. After that, the message is that there is no place like home. But, gee, a home is not necessarily a place. It's the loving people who surround you, putting a mantle of love around you. That's all you need."

But I also know that love is ephemeral, whimsical, changeable. As a journalist, I have witnessed love in many dimensions, complicated and circuitous. There are people I have interviewed who will never know how they erased some of my doubts that love exists, how they convinced me that love is available to those who don't close themselves off. These were the times that love found me even when I wasn't looking for it. And sometimes I felt cheated by love. People I thought of as friends, people I wanted to see socially as the result of an interview, showed me what I didn't want to know: that some people love the stories and not the storyteller.

$$\Diamond$$

SUSAN GOLDWATER was a stunning, curvaceous blond when I met her shortly after her marriage to then-California Rep. Barry Goldwater, Jr. She invited me to their charming Alexandria, Virginia, townhouse for coffee and the minute I saw the new Mrs. Goldwater, I liked her. She was a tall ray of blond sunshine, a woman glowing with the luminosity that is born of love fulfilled. Her eyes sparkled when she talked of her new husband. I did a story on the glamorous Mrs. Barry Goldwater, daughter-in-law of the elder Arizona senator, a statesman who adored her and would, in fact, prove to be her closest ally when she and his son were divorced.

We became friends. We often saw each other in Washington and we always seemed to be analyzing modern female lifestyles, how ambitious career women could still remain womanly—as if the pursuit of success somehow cancelled femaleness. These conversations were not for print. They were for us, two women trying to find a balance between the tilt of career versus the pull of a man. We were always trying to invent ways to hold ourselves steady on the seesaw of feminism and femininity.

Four years into the marriage, after the birth of Barry Goldwater III, the Goldwaters got a no-fault divorce. Susan Goldwater had a pilot's license, raced cars, remained lovely and WDVM–TV in Washington snapped her up to be co-host of "PM Magazine." It was widely rumored that she was being groomed for a network television job that would ultimately put her in competition with Jane Pauley and Phyllis George.

I went to Washington to do a second major story on Goldwater, a story about her divorce, about her switch from marriage to career, something we had talked about informally. We met for dinner at a little Georgetown bistro. The next day I telephoned my finished story to the *Globe.* When I hung up, the telephone rang and it was Goldwater, who was having second thoughts about our interview. She asked me to do something I have never done before in my professional life. She asked me to revise the story, redo it.

It was an embarrassing situation. It turned out that career was not Susan Goldwater's immediate priority, as I had written. A sixty-year-old millionaire from Cincinnati and Miami, Marvin Warner, then American ambassador to Switzerland, would soon be Goldwater's third husband. She had not told me this during our interview. Obviously she would be concentrating on being Mrs. Warner, not being a television star. This was something not easily explained to my discerning editors. My credibility would be challenged because I had trusted Goldwater as a friend a bit too completely, too soon.

Goldwater assured me that she was still career-oriented. The news of her impending marriage had been gossiped about in Washington newspapers but since this was to be her first official in-depth interview about it, I asked permission from my editors to do a second story, to kill the first one.

But this time I kept my distance. I realized that I had gotten too close to my subject and had lost my objectivity. This time I presented all sides of the Susan Goldwater odyssey. Washington friends had told me that many television hopefuls in the area felt they had been edged out by Goldwater, who had the "name" but no television experience. How she had been courted by Ted Forstmann of the famous fashion fabric house. How she tried to keep her relationship with her ex-husband "friendly" for the sake of their child. How she and Barry Goldwater kept running into each other at Washington parties and how Barry sarcastically introduced her to his date as "my wife," although they were divorcing and were mutually bitter.

I told the Goldwater story straight out, without sentimentality, and Goldwater thought it had a bitter twist. She told me so at her wedding reception to Ambassador Warner at his sprawling farm near downtown Cincinnati. A few months later, I heard that the Warners were divorcing and that's when Susan Goldwater and I became incommunicado. She never acknowledged my letters or my phone calls. I did not want to write a third story about a love gone wrong. I only wanted to know if she was all right. But our early friendship, which included a wonderful party she hosted for me at Senator Goldwater's Washington apartment, could not survive what she thought of as the unfair power of the pen.

$$\Diamond$$

WHAT FRUSTRATES me about love, even friendship-love, is its lack of perfection. What faces a journalist who makes journalism her life is that she finds herself loved only when she writes fluff. I have avoided that kind of journalism as earnestly as I have avoided bitchy journalism. Love can humanize an interview, make it a story anybody can understand. I write about real-life love stories, with all the complications, with special feelings. Maybe I still harbor a childish fantasy that love can make the worst things bearable, that it can somehow make wrong things right. It's an optimistic feeling that I need to share with readers.

I know this about love. If it is real, it can withstand the most terrible trials. True love does not die easily. It is a great natural power, an energy you can tap into, a stimulant that makes problems easier to solve. Love can't be bought, but it costs in time and sentiment because it has to be nourished. It's a cliché that love never runs smoothly. It never does. But it has a marvelous ability to turn itself around when people really want it to.

$$\Diamond$$

NEW YORK'S longest reigning senator, Jacob Javits, had just lost his treasured seat after twenty-four years to a relative unknown, Alfonse D'Amato on September 9, 1980. Javits was also losing his health, a seventy-seven-year-old man suffering from a degenerative motor sickness, Lou Gehrig's disease, which made walking and breathing a great struggle. Javits, ever a warrior, was never a man to weep in public. But I had asked to interview him on the subject of courage, how he was keeping his spirit alive while facing the depressing postscript of political defeat and, worse, a defeated body. He agreed to talk to me.

Javits was sitting forlornly in the paisley room of his East Side townhouse eating bland oatmeal from a metal tray served by a maid, rather than his wife, Marion, who had a bevy of attractive escorts at her beck and call. Javits was wearing a dark business suit, a starched white shirt, and regimental tie, as if he were going to the office. He was going nowhere, except eventually to a hospital to try experimental drugs, to become a kind of guinea pig.

His gnarled fingers fiddled with eyeglasses which he put on deliberately, slowly, to get a better look at me, his interviewer, someone he had known fleetingly in his earlier Washington days. His gaze became more insistent, more penetrating, and he was judging me as carefully as I was judging him.

We talked about his magnificent political career, about his tenth and final contest, an old soldier offering his age as experience and being rejected by the very party and the very public he had served. "I went to the well too often," Javits said, fighting to control his quivering voice. I sensed he had deep regrets. I saw it in the mournful look in eyes magnified by thickish glasses. I knew his great tug-of-war had been the pull of career against the love of his wife.

Always he had been silent on the marital subject. But his wife had been quoted everywhere when she expressed her caustic definition of their marriage: that Washington was her husband's wife and that she was merely his mistress.

It was not the sort of cutting quote a journalist could throw at an ailing old senator and expect a civil answer. But although Javits had always responded to his wife's now-legendary comment with no comment, I felt obliged to broach the subject. I knew this might be one of Javits's final interviews and his stormy marriage was part of his history. I wanted to be in on it.

I skipped into the subject lightly, rather than head-on. But I used a method that works when you're not sure your mutuality with the person being interviewed is intact. I asked three questions in rapid succession, questions that blurred together as a mini-speech. Purposely I did not ask a single question. It would have been too easy for Javits to dismiss it and me. When I posed the three questions, I added my own theories to the question, giving the inter-

rogation the added dimension of my reaction, my view, of
his situation. I hoped, indeed I gambled, that Javits would
treat my questions as challenges, kind ones. I hoped he
would be quick on the uptake.

This is what I asked:

"Did you ever miss your wife's presence in Washington, *where you needed her most?*

"Did you regret not having her as an *ally, as your
Washington hostess?*

"Did you regret she stayed in New York, *leading a
life separate and independent from yours?"*

There was a pause. Neither the senator nor I moved
a muscle. Then, slowly, he opened his mouth and he answered my three questions in three words: "Sure, sure,
sure." And it was as if the doors of his memory had opened
and then and there he seemed to make an extraordinary
decision.

Javits decided to use this interview, this conversation,
as a personal vehicle of public apology to his wife, who
had made a well-publicized life for herself in New York
without interfering with his in Washington. They never
divorced. Despite the storms, he was back in the old port,
his New York home, a place from which he had long been
absent.

The senator opened up on the subject of Marion, how
he had made his job his priority, how she played second
fiddle to his ambitions. He told me that now, in retrospect,
politics had obsessed and possessed him until it became
what he called "the irresistible target of my life." Javits
regretted that he had not balanced his career with love.

The interview moved rapidly, almost of its own volition. I hardly needed to steer it. It was as if Javits were
happy to relate the flaws of his love story, to admit to them,
the recapitulation being his way of righting the wrong.
I didn't even have to ask a whole question. I'd utter a
phrase and the senator would snatch it like a hungry man,
finish it.

"If you had to do it over again . . ."

"Yes, if I had it to do over again, I'd make better accommodations with New York. I don't think I decided enough points in favor of my family, my wife. Too often I decided the question of my presence on the public side, not the private one. A city career could have led to the mayoralty. If I had to do it over again, I would inventory the idea of running for the mayor of New York. . . . I did not take opportunity of *that* opportunity."

"Was it your wife's loyalty that . . ."

"Yes, yes, it was partially my wife's loyalty to me, which was very real. Partially it was my own determination. I am persistent. I adhered to the determination that I could make the marriage work. I was not easily discouraged, not easily thrown off. *But I didn't do enough in terms of contribution to the marriage itself.*"

"Did job-related stresses put stress on your marriage and . . ."

"We expect too much of politicians. We literally tear them to bits. They're supposed to be in a suburban county, say in New York, and, at exactly the same moment, they're expected to be in Washington. You cannot be in two places at one time. But you've *got* to be in two places at one time. Or else a resentment builds up . . . and we stretch ourselves thin, and when we get home, we're expected to be of sweet disposition, relaxed. But you can't maintain this sweetness if your life is being lived in a political fracas."

"What about Marion's view of Washington? . . ."

"Washington doesn't have the excitement of New York. It doesn't have the cosmopolitanism of New York. Washington does not have an openness of thought. It is not receptive to innovation. There is only one key employer, the government. That is not a good thing."

These were painful revelations. As a woman, I was moved by the frankness of this man who loved a woman enough to ask forgiveness in print, to admit his shortcomings as a husband and, importantly, to echo his wife's opinion of Washington, the city he served and loved more than her. As a journalist, I was touched that Javits would entrust me with the delivery of this tardy romantic apology. He put his feelings in my hands and made no fancy speeches, issued no warnings about accuracy. There was a feeling of trust between the senator and me, something I would never abuse.

After the Senator Javits story appeared, I got a warm handwritten letter from Marion Javits. She said what I knew, that this was the first time her husband had opened up publicly about their strained relationship, the first time he had echoed her sentiments about Washington. It was the letter of a woman who still loved her man, a woman moved by the fact that her husband had, in the last days of his life, admitted errors of decision regarding her.

$$\Diamond$$

LOVING MEANS leaving yourself open to receive love in whatever form it comes. Even in interviews. There has to be some give and take in the game of questions and answers. To attain a sense of mutuality, you have to leave yourself open, even become vulnerable. This is a tricky, tightrope approach because you do what you've been told not to do: You get involved with your subject.

Ray Charles, blind since childhood, suddenly grasped my left wrist with his right hand. Then he stretched his index finger until it rested firmly on my pulse. He had a moody expression on his ebony face. His head was cocked to one side, as if he were straining to hear something beyond the extension of my heartbeat. He didn't break this spell of intense concentration until he heard what he wanted to hear, my "inner vibrations."

Only then did he ask me to sit with him on the big black grand piano in the dimly lit inner sanctum of his Los Angeles studio. It was clear that what Ray Charles could not see he could sense by the duality of touch and ears honed to a compensating sensitivity. When I spoke, he listened to my *tone* as carefully as he considered my words. I asked Charles what a blind man can see. He wasn't shocked by the question which, to some, might seem stupid.

He talked about "visualization," about sensing a room, about imagining people. I wanted to know the specifics of visualization, the details. What I really wanted to know was how Ray Charles, blind since five from glaucoma, orphaned when he was fifteen, the same year he entered show business, conquered blindness rather than let blindness conquer him.

That question brought out the real story, a story about love. Ray Charles was spurred by something his mother had told him, something she said sharply in the name of love, something intuitive to goad him past his cage of darkness. "You're blind, not stupid," she said. Ray Charles believed her with all his heart and that influence, born of love, became his credo.

I told him that I, too, had a mother who believed I *could* when there wasn't a reason in the world to back her sentiment. He heard me. But he didn't acknowledge my comment that faith of this magnitude is based on pure love because it refuses to acknowledge limitations. He understood. Ray Charles then drew me a parallel situation from his life. He assumed that I would understand that he understood what I had said about the power of love.

"Baby," he began, "I never see no one else use a seeing eye dog or a white cane. I'm the type of cat who likes to do things as close to normal. I got blind when I was five. My mom, she told me: 'There are two ways to do things now. You've got to find the *other* way.' She was talking about getting around just like everyone else. By myself."

He told me his mother had a fourth-grade education, maybe fifth-, but that she had great wisdom. She was a stark realist who leveled with her little boy who was going blind. And sometimes she went hungry to make sure he had

enough to eat. Most of all, she loved him enough to convince him he could cope and then she showed him how.

"We'd go to a strange place," he said. "She'd take me
all around the room, showing me everything. Then she'd
say: 'Get it?' After that, she'd show me nothing. If I walked
into a table, if I fell, she wouldn't warn me. I just fell. I
know that killed her. When I picked myself up, she'd say:
'I ain't always gonna be around to tell you, 'Stop.' Even
your friends won't have time for you. Do as much as you
can for yourself.' That's what I done. Another thing about
mom. She told me the truth ninety-five percent of the time.
The only thing not true was about food. There was a little
food sometimes and she wasn't eating. But I didn't know.
I didn't know *those* were the lies."

They were lies of love, magnificent ones.

$$\Diamond$$

PEOPLE HAVE told me unbelievable stories about the power
of love. I believed them because I know that love, if it has
depth, is a connection that knows no boundaries. It is
possible to communicate with someone you love in your
dreams or have him or her communicate with you. I have
had that experience. There's a boundlessness to love, as if
it could sear through geography and be beamed from one
person to another under the most extreme circumstances.
This aspect of love cannot be explained. The fact that it
happens is its own testimony to the capacity of love.

Through no fault of his own, Barry Rosen was where
he didn't want to be, in a maximum security jail cell, a
victim of outrageous political circumstances that assumed
world proportions. Rosen was one of fifty-two American
hostages held captive for fourteen months, until January,
1981. He thought he would go mad and he also thought
about suicide. Enmired in a deep depression, he had heart
palpitations, serious insomnia.

At first he treated his captors arrogantly, taunting them with idle threats. His protests, a foolish show of false superiority, got him in handcuffs. His attitude changed. Rosen became silent, withdrew within himself, had the blank stare of introspection. It was as if he was asleep all day, blocking out the awfulness of his reality.

I met Rosen and his wife, Barbara, a Cher lookalike, in New York after his release. I conducted two separate interviews, one totally independent of the other. Neither knew what the other had said to me. Much to my surprise, when I analyzed my interview notes, I discovered that although the Rosens had been separated by half a world, their feelings and independent decisions about how to handle their reaction to the hostage situation converged almost simultaneously. At the exact time Rosen had retreated into his shell of silence, his wife had long fits of sleep.

She told me: "I blocked it out. People would say: 'What do you feel?' Well, I didn't feel a thing. I was immobilized completely. I slept fifteen hours a day. This went on for four months."

He told me: "My body was in total fear but my mind was saying, 'Hold on.' In this nervous situation, it is flight or fight. I could do neither. So I slowed down. I went inward."

Occasionally each received the other's letters. Since the mail was censored, there was no exchange of news, just mutual reassurances of love. Each didn't know how the other was reacting to the letters but it was the same for both of them.

She told me: "I'd get a letter. When you don't hear, you go on. Death is easier to deal with. Somebody dies and it's over. A letter is like pouring salt in old wounds."

He told me: "When letters came, my heart would pump. It was hard for me to stay unconcerned. These were the moments I was hyper. I put the letters under my pillow. The letters highlighted the separation."

The Rosens were having strikingly similar reactions to

captivity and to their meager connection, the letters. They were reacting as if they were one. They were even in perfect stride later, when the urge to cope hit them at the same time.

Rosen described turning the corner: "I know I reached a point beyond crisis, a point where I decided I wanted to live. There is no criteria for captivity, no lessons on how not to be a coward. So I went inward and provided my own criteria. That criteria was to be *self-reliant,* to say to myself: 'I can handle stress.' I did not get strong or develop more muscle. I simply became less judgmental about myself and I survived."

He made the decision to take responsibility for himself, to study, to do calisthenics, to try to move beyond the limits of prison. Rosen changed his attitude, became more confident, self-determined. So did Barbara. Just as her husband discovered his own strengths, she gave up her sleep retreat. She veered into action, becoming vocal and visible, swinging away from inertia.

She went to Europe to meet West German Chancellor Helmut Schmidt, French President Valery Giscard d'Estaing, and the Pope. "I didn't want to sit around or sleep or cry," she told me. "I wanted to turn things around." Her husband was already doing the same thing for himself, by himself.

The Rosens' love put them on the same wavelength. Barry Rosen told me he survived the terrible insecurity and boredom of captivity by concentrating on remembered moments of married love. He ran them like reels through his memory machine, freezing certain pictures into a single frame, imagining he was actually there, in the picture, with his wife. This was his "vision." Hers was actually fighting for her husband's release, a vision of being reunited, and they were.

◇

YOLANDA KING, oldest child of Dr. Martin Luther King, Jr., has visions of her late father. They come to her in flashes of clarity. Her father, a 1964 Nobel Prize winner, was assassinated in Memphis on April 4, 1968. But his image is so strong, so loving, that whenever she panics, or is frightened, he "appears" and the fear disappears. King, an actress and activist who graduated from Smith College and New York University, told me she had a vision of her father the day before my interview with her. She had been standing at a podium at Wheaton College, about to make a speech. Her throat tightened, her heart raced. "I thought I was going to collapse," she said. But, in her mind's eye, she "saw" her father and was flooded with a feeling of calm, peace. Yolanda King was talking about the power of love and those feelings extended into the next day and it seeped into our interview, over lunch at Boston's Ritz-Carlton Hotel.

The vision of her father was so hauntingly real that she related it to me with ease, telling me that she felt her father's presence between us even as we talked. I cannot say I saw what she saw. But I felt her father's presence, his love, through her because she reflected it. She pulsated with energy. Her aura was positive, her eyes sparkled, her words were eloquent.

King traced her "visions" to her father's funeral at the Ebenezer Baptist Church in Atlanta, a grieving twelve-year-old child too stunned to accept the reality of the sudden, cruel death of the father she adored.

This is the story that King told me:

"For two years after my daddy's death, I dreamed of him every night, all the things we had done together. I dreamed he really didn't leave me. That he was away participating in a struggle somewhere. In my dreams, we were allowed to see him once a year and, when we did, there was a big feast, the house was full of folk. Then gradually, the dreams changed. We had to go to him. He would not come to us. So we went to him and we had to go underground. It was damp, the ground. There were little sections and in one section there was my father. We could not just go and visit there. Then, little by little, the visits got less frequent and the dreams ended.

"That's how I got over daddy's death. That's how I fully accepted it. The reason I didn't go crazy is that I had the dream. *He was there.* It was so real. We always did lots of things together. We used to swim together and daddy was always nice enough to let me beat him. I dreamed often we went swimming. I woke up disappointed that it had only been a dream. But I was being healed. My daddy's consciousness was coming to me, aiding me."

When Yolanda King talked to me of her dreams, her link to her loved one, her dead father, could I dismiss it lightly as childish fantasy? The inner core of all of us is the heart, the love in it. To be allowed to see that love, to talk about it, is a privilege I take seriously. My own search for love has helped me let go of my own inhibitions, to be open and empathetic to loving situations related to me by other people.

Once I, too, had a silent dream, a wordless slow-motion dream. I will remember it forever. I was walking slowly down a hospital corridor, as if dazed. A nurse saw me coming and pointed to the last room at the end of the hall, the one on the left.

I went into the small cubicle and lying helplessly on a crumpled bed pushed up against a barred window was my brother. One leg was in traction. The other leg was in a hip cast. His bare chest, his arms were badly bruised and scratched. He seemed to be in horrible pain but bore it the way he always bore pain, as a fine soldier. He was attending Vermont's Norwich University when it had the same curriculum as West Point. But now his face was twisted and he was perspiring. In the dream he smiled when he saw me approach his bed, a weak smile as if even that hurt.

The night of my dream, my brother, one leg in a hip cast from a sports accident, was actually in a terrible auto crash. He was pinned in the front passenger seat of a car that twisted around a tree. The bone of his other leg was so badly crushed that, eventually, a pin had to be inserted in it to heal, something which took two major operations. When the pin was finally removed, it turned out to be a long steel rod. The pain of inserting it and removing it was horrendous.

The next morning when I went to the hospital, it was the corridor of my dream, the cubicle of my dream, the exact scene of my dream. My brother, now a bank president, smiled at me in the same wan way. Even a nurse pointed to the same direction, the same room as in my dream.

$$\Diamond$$

ON ANOTHER HOT summer's day, I was summoned abruptly into an antiseptic-smelling hospital corridor and matter of factly told by a doctor, an indistinct man who wore gray and spoke in a hushed monotone, that the days of my mother's life were reduced to a few weeks.

The ash colored voice announced that three operations in the zigzag course of the last year were useless. Time had run out. The cancer had spread. My mother had existed with the painful evidence of her mortality, those awful scars that slashed across one side of her beautiful body to the other.

She knew I was being told the devastating news. When I returned to her room, she was sitting calmly in a chair facing the door. She was waiting to give me all she had left of the last remnants of our life together: her love.

It was she, a dying woman, who comforted me, a living one. Our eyes were locked in mutual pain. She, a stoic, didn't cry. It was I who sobbed. When I sunk to the floor by her slippered feet, when I put my head in her lap, when I buried my face in the folds of her pink robe, she patted my head and let me cry. But not for long.

My mother was a valiant woman who always believed that time was of the essence, that time was a precious commodity not to be wasted. She had always used time well, always speaking in blunt sheaths, always getting to the truth of things, something I've always tried to do in my stories. She never wasted time pussyfooting around a point. She came to it. One last time she told me what she had always emphasized: never allow anybody to do my thinking for me. She told me to be an original and to be happy in my originality, to expect nothing of it except the joy of originality itself.

She believed, as I do, that independence is what makes you free. She warned me never to be caged again. She told me the worst cages were the ones I would make for myself. Once I made a decision, she said, stand by it. She told me to leave a little room for mistakes but never to make the same mistake twice. Then she patted my head gently and told me everything would be all right.

She became very tired and I helped a nurse put her to bed. And there, on her deathbed, she held onto life by a wispy thread, her love for me holding death at bay. Love is what made her last four months instead of a few weeks.

Silently she waited for me every day. I sat at the foot of her bed, writing columns in longhand. This daily scene was her last assurance that my life as a journalist, the life we had shared, was continuing even if she was not. This was our last love communion, a sharing of her final days. We loved each other enough to pretend that everything was normal. We made believe that nothing had changed for us except the place of our daily get-together, her hospital room.

Death was in that room, invading the nostrils with its foul smell. But love was there, too, and ultimately it would make her death bearable. I denied my mother's death with steely vehemence. I pleaded with God to spare her, work a miracle, reverse the irreversible. Slowly, she shrank, actually getting smaller, more girllike. Once she tried to take herself to the bathroom, to feel a sense of dignity about her natural body functions. She had fallen along the way and had to be lifted back to bed by two orderlies. I watched her daily survival by intravenous feeding. I saw the portions become slower, less frequent. She was being weaned from life before my eyes.

Late one November night, a night when the winds whistled through trees etched like black lace against the sky, I talked to God in a way I never had, nor, I think, ever will again. I stared up at earth's star-studded roof and told God it was all right to take my mother now. I spoke as if I, not He, were in control. And God let me get away with that. He let me feel I had the power to release her to Him. She died a few hours later.

There was to be no wake, except for her children. My mother had planned her own funeral, even picking her own burial spot. On her deathbed, holding my hand, she asked me to execute the details alone and, in a trance of mourning, I did so. When she died, I went alone to the funeral home, to the little corner room in which my mother lay in her final sleep, dressed in the impeccable beige-gray suit we had bought together in New York. I had chosen her burial clothes. My mother looked beautiful, very young, glowing in death, perhaps the last joy at being released finally from pain. I touched the body, shocked that it was marble-cold, like a museum statue.

Hanging from my mother's neck was a silver necklace with the number *one*. I had surprised my mother with it one Saturday, no occasion, kissing her, telling her she'd always be Number One with me.

$$\diamond$$

I NEVER thought of red as a serene color. But one spring day I met Dr. Norman Vincent Peale, the famous rector of the Marble Collegiate Church, New York, one of America's greatest preachers. We sat together in his Fifth Avenue office, a vermillion cocoon that had an aura of great serenity. This peaceful eighty-three-year-old man, the espouser of positive thinking power, dominated the red room as we talked of love in simple human parables. Dr. Peale said that people sometimes forget that love has great healing properties, that it is nature's medicine, that everyone is born with the capacity to love. He also told me that people are always asking him how to express love and that it's not always what you say *but what you do.*

He told me this story about a friend who extended love to him when he needed it most. But his friend never used the word, love. His friend acted lovingly.

Dr. Peale's mother, whom he adored, died on a Saturday. The next day, Sunday, he had a speaking engagement in another state. "I loved my mother dearly," he said, "I asked the Lord: 'Do I have what it takes to speak?' I thought I heard my mother say, 'Don't moon around. Do your job.' So I went to the train and into the car came a friend of mine, a big, burly fellow, a colonel. We said hello. He asked me where I was going. I told him I was on my way to preach a sermon. He said he was going to a clambake.

"After a while, the colonel said: 'What's the matter with you? You're not acting like yourself.' I told him my mother had died. He didn't say a word. When we got to his stop, he didn't get off. 'Why?' I asked him. He told me he decided not to go to the clambake, that since it was Sunday, he felt he should come to church to listen to me preach.

"Well, after church, he took me to lunch and, after that, to the train. Before saying good-bye, he said: 'You've seen me through some tough ones. God sent me along to be with you today.' That's all he said. And he walked off. My friend didn't say: 'I'm sorry. I know how much you loved your mother. Good-bye.' He just stayed there and was my *loving* friend."

I don't know why, but Dr. Peale, a scholar who graduated from Ohio Wesleyan and Boston University, turned the tables on me. For no reason, he asked me about my mother who had not entered the interview. I told him she was dead but alive in my heart and in my mind. I tried not to cry. But I did. And Dr. Peale, who had never before met me, a journalist who had come to talk to him about the link between attitude and success, cried with me.

I never told Dr. Peale this but I felt that in some strange way, my mother had pushed me into his presence. I had been mourning nonstop, going through life like a sleep-walker, hurting inside. I needed reassurance badly and Dr. Peale reached out and gave it to me. All in an interview about love.

THE
FAME FACTOR

STEADY STRANDS of rain and whipping winds were turning umbrellas inside out. On such a dismal Monday, when the fog plays hide and seek with the gray landscape, I boarded an Eastern shuttle flight to La Guardia.

Due to bad weather conditions, the plane was an hour late and an aged man who had been carried on and strapped into the seat next to mine lost control of his bladder and, without fully realizing it, sat in his own urine, mumbling incoherently and pointing to his watch.

At La Guardia taxis were scarce, a major rainy day problem in New York, forcing grudging gratitude for the usual uncivilized ride into Manhattan. My hotel room was an amusing testimony to a lovers' evening. Her side of the rumpled bed had blood stains on the sheet and purple lipstick marks on the rim of a half-filled brandy glass. He was a Marlboro man, judging from the empty cigarette pack sitting next to a drained brandy glass.

Celebrity is not necessarily what you are. It's how other people perceive you and what you do. There are those who believe that a journalist's life is a celebrity's life—that my own life is no different from that of the personalities I interview. Yet that is often the furthest thing from the truth. These typical bits of drama were the prelude to a confirmed interview with "Chips" television star, Erik Estrada, once the romantic interest of the former Mrs. Vidal Sassoon and the heartthrob of millions of women who swoon at the sound of his name, which is really Enrique. He had the makings of a good rags-to-riches story, so we arranged to meet in New York.

Estrada grew up tough on the streets of Spanish Harlem, where he shined shoes. But Estrada got famous playing Ponch, the motorcycle cop in the NBC-TV series. Now he was in the news because he left the show in a huff over his returns of claimed ownership of twenty-five percent of "Chips" and he had just settled the suit with MGM for $12 million, over three years. Not only did he have fame, he had fortune. Estrada was then driving a sleek white Rolls-Royce and living in high style in Beverly Hills, in sharp contrast to his ghetto upbringing.

While waiting too long for Estrada at the appointed time and place, I was paged by telephone. A crisp female voice told me that he had just cancelled the interview. The telephone voice, now decidedly bored, didn't know if the interview could be rearranged. She took the attitude that we were dealing with Estrada, *star,* a state of rarefied being meant to imply that it was the *star* who called the shots. Not me. Women who protest shabby treatment are labeled bitches, and although I felt like being bitchy, I controlled myself, which gave me a migraine headache.

After flying back to Boston, *without* the interview and with a day's precious deadline lost, the Erik Estrada interview was suddenly rescheduled. Only now it was Saint Patrick's Day, not a holiday to invade New York City, especially Fifth Avenue. Estrada's office left a message not to worry, a car with a driver who knew the "short cuts" would take me from La Guardia to the interview scene. It's rare for me to accept a limousine ride, but I knew I had to save time.

So it was back to New York, same hotel, same time, different day. Only now Estrada added insult to injury by

being over two hours late. The photographer, Tom Mid-
dlemiss, a charming Irishman who wished he were shoot-
ing on the streets, waited the hours with me and commented frequently, as I seethed, that I had the patience of
a saint. Not true: I was really waiting to tell off this pretty
boy called Erik Estrada.

Little did I know that Estrada would eventually arrive
with a musclebound bodyguard whose tallness was a visual
distraction and an attractive female publicist who made
me laugh when she apologized for the lateness with the
excuse that *their* driver didn't know the "short cuts" and
was held up in traffic.

Estrada, a remarkably handsome man of Puerto Rican
extraction, ignored my quick critique of his social behavior. As I sputtered, he led me calmly by the elbow to a
quiet interview spot where we talked about the impact of
"ego energy," the phrase he used to describe the powers
to be gleaned from judicious use of self-confidence. Estrada
treated my own anger with a sense of forced politeness and
remarkable shrewdness, switching my negative attack on
what I perceived to be his overblown ego into the positive
use of ego, something he thought he had proved.

The interview was moving along, reaching a cres-
cendo, when it suddenly fell flat on its face.

A breathtakingly beautiful blond slipped onto the scene,
slithered into a chair across from Estrada and did nothing
except stare at him passionately through a marvelous fringe
of meticulous false black eyelashes. She was apparently his
amour of the moment, perhaps the woman who had cost
me two trips to New York, the "other" woman who had
taken up my appointed time. Their eyes seemed to trade
great waves of sexual excitement that excluded everyone
else. It was this intense private communication that ended
the interview. It was, in fact, an incredibly romantic scene
that made its way into the lead of my story.

◇

NOT ALL celebrities treat journalists so shabbily. The more educated the person, the more polished the interview, regardless of the extenuating circumstances. Fame is best when it is not flaunted. Only the most sophisticated, most secure people handle fame with humility, as if it were a gift on loan, like love.

In November of 1981, James A. Baker III, Texas lawyer, a man of high intensity markedly different from Estrada, was using his best courtroom manner to juggle a difficult situation. A long-confirmed interview with me was unexpectedly coinciding with the final, dramatic moments of the AWACS vote. Baker, President Ronald Reagan's chief of staff, could have cancelled the interview as nonchalantly as Estrada did. Baker had a more legitimate reason. But he let me pass through the White House gates, allowed me to be ushered into his splendid office next to the Oval Office. Baker was sitting next to a battery of push-button telephones, facing my questions against the pull, the drama, of the AWACS vote, which, at these very moments, was coming into focus as still another major Reagan victory.

I understood Baker's dilemma. He was the president's buffer, a man using his influence to influence the big votes. I was an interruption, a distraction, not even a member of the Washington press corps. But he gamely answered my pointed questions about the controversy surrounding Secretary of State Alexander Haig, a man who seemed endlessly embroiled in a behind-the-scenes power struggle, and about Nancy Reagan—not a hit with the press herself. Baker weaved in and out of the interview to make crucial calls minutes before the president's victorious announcement. He juggled the AWACS vote and my interview with memorable sophistication.

Baker even managed to personalize the excitement of the moment with telling introspection: "This job," he said, his hand on the receiver of a direct telephone line to Reagan, "is based on twenty-twenty *hindsight*. Everything you do is open to close scrutiny. After it's over, you ask ques-

tions. Did I wait too long? Not long enough? Why did I do
what I did?" He was talking about the demands and responsibilities of fame by association, wondering if he had
performed well in the fishbowl existence of the White
House. Fame does not allow you to fail in private.

His mind was on AWACS but he allowed me to watch
him go to still another telephone, the one with the direct
line to the CIA. Baker barked into the receiver: "The sta-
bility of the regime report?" He put question marks into a
declarative statement—a kind of conversational shorthand
designed to keep secret things secret. "Let's use that right
now," he said with great authority and hung up.

Baker allowed me to witness history being made. Outside, at the White House gates, I had passed a horde of
print and television reporters huddled together, anxiously
awaiting the outcome of the vote. But I was the one inside
the White House, next to Baker as AWACS came into being.
I left only when it was time for Baker himself to leave his
office, to leave the White House, to go to the president
who was, indeed, about to make a victory statement about
AWACS. Baker was even gentleman enough to apologize
that he had given me less time than he had promised.

Here was a man who saw fame as a responsibility to
be used carefully. Baker did not pursue fame. It fell in his
lap, mostly because of Nancy Reagan's influence. He was
her choice for the job. He treated his ex-officio fame as a
communications tool. Instead of using the pressing immediacy of the moment to shut me out, to erect a barrier,
Baker included me. He gambled on my reportorial imagination to capture that moment of history.

Estrada saw fame as celebrity, as if the two were synonymous. Fame, to him, was a force that could be translated
into money and, to Estrada, money was the best security
of all. Without fame, without money, he did not even feel
well physically. "I just wanted to get rid of the sick feeling
of poorness," he told me. "That's what poor feels like, *sick.*
And I've gotten over that feeling."

I didn't believe Estrada when he said that. He never
offered me so much as a cup of tea although the interview
was at New York's Ritz-Carlton Jockey Club lounge. Fame
filled an emotional void for Estrada, a substitute for personal forms of validation. I believed that, especially when
he told me that his parents were divorced when he was
two and that he never felt adequately loved. He and his
mother, now on a generous allowance from her famous
son, were welfare recipients. The power of having money
was something he learned early. At age five, Estrada "helped"
sell ice cream cones. He describes that experience as his
"first job." Later, when he shined shoes, he had to defend
himself from gang bullies who would beat him up without
provocation. He told me he quickly learned the "advan-
tages of hitting first." He wasn't scared of physical beatings
because he could fight back. He was scared of what he felt
inside.

"As a kid," he told me, "the first thing I learned in the
category of 'fears' is that I might never have financial freedom. So I set out to conquer that fear, to have financial
independence. That has always been my motivating force.
This business of my 'ego' has been misunderstood. What
they [MGM and NBC–TV] didn't know was this: I'd fight
anybody who tried to take a nickel from me illegally.

"See, what my enemies fought was that old fear. They
forgot I was a kid from the street. I'm a fighter. I've always
been hungry. But not for food. I've got a hunger for a strong
self-image, a hunger for respect. I've always been motivated
by one thing: to clear up, no, to *clean* up my own insecurities about money. I thought: I want to get rid of my
childhood stigma, poorness. I had a clean shirt. I wasn't
hungry. But we were poor."

Then Estrada delivered a soliloquy on money with a
passion that seemed to send electricity into his dark gypsy
eyes. I took down every word.

"Money gives you space. I look at it this way. If you
earn $100 in one hour versus $100 in ten hours, you've

got nine hours to yourself. I chose acting because of what it could do for me from a financial viewpoint. People always asked me: 'Why do you want to be a star?' Stardom never entered the picture. I never seriously considered the star stuff. I figured if I could be on television regularly, I'd be making good money.

"I'd rather be rich than rich and famous. The rag sheets print things about me that are not true. I've read that I'm 'spoiled.' Well, nobody spoiled me. I've earned everything I've got. People say: 'Look at him. Look at what he's *got.*' I'd like to have money and I'd like to have *privacy.* I don't. But, in a way, I've lucked out. Poor people can point to me and say, 'Hey, look, he came out of Harlem.' That's the point of fame."

$$\diamondsuit$$

CELEBRITY can be a kind of mass love, a compensation for the real thing. It does not always require great standards of excellence. You can get famous for being interesting or bizarre. Jimmy Connors and John McEnroe, two magnificent tennis players, have not cramped their controversial personal style; indeed, their colorfulness has added to the great public interest in them which, in turn, translates into annual fortunes of somewhere between $3 and $5 million. Both are exhibitionists. Connors is famous for his streetwise antics. McEnroe spits.

Whatever the cause of fame, the effect is the same. It individualizes you. But journalistic fame is recognition from a distance. It is there but it doesn't touch you in a personal way. There's an open space between you and your public. Your lives touch vicariously, through your stories. That kind of indistinct fame has always magnetized me. To be a name, a by-line, without a face or distinguishable persona, means being able to observe without being observed. It is a great advantage, something like a one-way mirror which

allows you to see without being seen. It is arm's length
approval, no strings, the connection indirect. It is *comfortable* fame. It carries with it no great responsibilities.

And, of course, it doesn't really work.

Only true celebrity is a door-opener. It gets other
celebrities to respond to your knock because, after all, you
are equals. Celebrity brings with it an automatic, innate
respect among other celebrities who take your telephone
calls. To be famous is to be part of a clique, to be set
apart as someone special in a small, select crowd of other
specials. It gives you a place, a sense of belonging. Fame
is a necessary tool of success because it puts your success
in the public eye where it gathers momentum and drives
you forward. It gives success constancy.

As for myself, I have a love-hate attitude toward fame.
Instant recognition, the *ultimate* fame, has a certain insid-
iousness to it. You have to be obsessed by it, be willing
not only to produce fame, but *reproduce* it over and over.
Fame isn't useful to a career unless it continues. It makes
demands on you. I've never been able to give fame everything I've got.

Andy Warhol once observed that "in the future everyone will be famous for fifteen minutes." He meant if you
are outrageous enough, people will notice. But the impact
will be temporary. *Real* fame has to last, be productive,
work in tandem with your career itself. What I don't like
about fame is that it is as much of a commitment as the
work itself. You can't be famous and put the pursuit of fame
on the back burner. You have to be "on" all the time.
Sometimes I like to turn life off, float aimlessly, dress slop-
pily, eat with my fingers, go without lipstick. You can't
enjoy these "ordinary" privileges and be famous.

Barbara Walters entered Orsini's, a chic mid-Manhat-
tan restaurant, at 1:30 one day. The restaurant, which caters
to a cross-section of socialites and fashionables, was jammed
to capacity. I watched her make a deliberate grand entrance.

She poised herself, as if she were walking on a runway and, chin held high, eyes straight ahead, walked smartly to her seat, never looking right or left. A small smile curled her lips into an expression of self-confidence. No one *seemed* to notice. But everyone *did.* Successful New Yorkers pretend to be blasé about other successful New Yorkers. But they're not. Barbara Walters did not let her mask of celebrity slip. The truly famous never can.

Fame can happen anywhere, but it is best when it happens in New York. Fame born elsewhere, whatever the circumstance, seems scant unless it is somehow sanctioned in New York *by* New York. The song says if you can make it there, you can make it anywhere. Which means "anywhere" is not as good as New York.

The communications world is Manhattan-centered and in the intensity of miles of corporate skyscraper headquarters, the *Boston Globe* seems hopelessly suburban. I know what it's like to be treated as an awkward out-of-towner. Not untypical is the question asked me by former Bostonian Pat Collins, now entertainment critic of the CBS–TV Morning News and author of a book about her own "niceness," a colleague whom I met unexpectedly when she was breakfasting with the late Martha Mitchell. "What are *you* doing here?" she queried when I said hello. The presence of a Boston journalist in New York seemed to her to be out of context, although I am in New York every few days. Another typical response is the closing line of people I've interviewed who live in New York. "If you ever get to New York again, call me," they say, as if a non-New York journalist in New York were a rarity, as if I were a *visitor.* If I had been an honest-to-goodness celebrity I would not have to explain the details of my career, how it works and how *I* work.

One of the most exciting men I have ever interviewed is Washingtonian Alex Orfila, ex-secretary general of the Organization of Amerian States, a millionaire horseman whose Argentinian family amassed a wine fortune. He was

ambassador to the United States under Juan Perón and was
known as the "ultimate" diplomat. Orfila, a former escort
of Jacqueline Kennedy Onassis before he married Helga,
an ex-model who had once been linked to Frank Sinatra,
blinked hard when he saw me the first time. "*You're* from
Boston?" he asked surprised, as if all Boston women were
legendary wearers of sneakers, "attic" clothes, and inherited hats.

We laughed at his blurted question, became friends
and dated when he was still single. Later, when I went to
the White House to interview Rosalynn Carter, Orfila ordered one of his chauffeured limousines, with diplomatic
license plates, to take me to the interview. It was a showy
move, the long, black shiny car suggesting that I was linked
to inside Washington, which I wasn't. Orfila and I were
platonic friends. But the uniformed guards at the White
House gates responded with efficient, respectful alacrity.
The gates flew open. The car was ushered forth with a
fine flourish. Usually journalists arrive at the White House
gates on foot and linger there on the sidewalk, regardless
of the weather, while their credentials are telephone-checked
by guards in boxes tucked behind those closed gates.

Orfila, an adventurous man who has a $3 million, 400-
acre horse farm in Middleburg, Virginia, and would sometimes come to Boston for lunch, knew something that he
wanted to teach me. Fame is an *illusion*. It can be created
with the proper trappings. What he later discovered, quite
by chance, is that illusions surrounding journalists are flimsy
and easily shattered. When a journalist isn't as celebrated
as the celebrities she writes about, she is subject to attack.
That was the lession *I* taught *him*.

He had invited me to a private Georgetown club, Pisces,
a dimly lit underground place then partly owned by Bob
Hope's nephew, Peter Malatesta. The occasion was a cocktail reception to honor then-Sen. Birch Bayh, an ambitious
presidential hopeful. Earlier I had published a piece on
Mrs. Bayh, "Marvella." I didn't know she thought my story

was anything but marvelous. During the interview she had told me she bought her clothes wholesale, which is roughly half the retail price. I put that fact in the story, never dreaming she would take offense. Mrs. Bayh imagined that this disclosure suggested she had made a deal with certain designers. If she dropped their names to the press, if she got them publicity, the exchange of favor could be construed to be the reason for the cut price. She thought this tainted her fame, made her seem less than wholesome. At the time, however, it was commonplace for celebrities to buy clothes wholesale, directly from the manufacturer or designer, rather than a store. Betty Ford certainly made no secret of her penchant for Albert Capraro's designs.

In Pisces, in full view of her husband who was motioning for her to stop, she lambasted me loudly. When I told her that everything was on record during an interview, she got louder. She damned the press in general and me in particular. I allowed Mrs. Bayh to have her tantrum. But I felt terribly embarrassed, as if I were the center of a facsimile television ad, the one where when E. F. Hutton talks, everybody listens. Certainly the Washington Propers at the party all standing around, drinks in hand, overheard the tirade. I saw that I was the subject of pro-and-con twitters, as if the partygoers were taking sides. It was a dismal, ghastly evening and I couldn't wait to leave.

Later that evening Orfila told me that I should have defended myself more spiritedly. We sat together talking in his car, parked in front of the Watergate Hotel, where I was staying. He asked me if I didn't know how to fight back, defend myself. I was silent and moody. Orfila then told me that I had been too nice. He said that niceness is sometimes mistaken for weakness or, worse, naiveté. He spoke to me as a caring friend, but he was scolding me, too. I told him that I let Mrs. Bayh have the upper hand because I knew how sick she was, that she was dying of cancer. Orfila squeezed my hand. We never spoke of this again.

But I thought to myself then and many times since: It would be better to be Barbara Walters.

She has the kind of fame that insulates her. She has *exalted* fame, the kind that puts her on equal footing with the people she interviews. I have never heard of Barbara Walters being openly attacked at private parties. She is criticized in print, and reporters harp on her lisp, which I always thought gave her style because she seemed to rise above it. Critics have preyed upon her sometimes-silly questions and off-putting abrasiveness, calling her, among other things, a sugar-coated cobra. She has winced, also in print. But nothing has stopped Barbara Walters in any way. She is *protected* by her fame, which she wears like a mantle. Her fame gives her automatic endurance.

Once, sitting with Barbara Walters in her surprisingly small ABC–TV office in New York, I asked her how she viewed her fame. Walters's answer suggested that she had a yearning to occasionally escape the rigors of fame, relax her image, be herself. She said poignantly: "I'd like life, *my* life, to be sweeter. The world is harsh. I'd like my own island somewhere. I'm interested in the quality of life." She has *quantity,* a $1-million-a-year job, and she has discovered that fame, for all its positiveness, makes people jealous of you. Once you reach a certain pinnacle, people seem to want to knock you down.

Barbara Walters and I do the same kind of work. We are, however, on opposite sides, separated by the fame factor. Walters's visibility through the medium of television has made her a household name. Newspapering is a business that hides its stars behind inanimate by-lines. People don't usually know what writers look like. Once I went to a polo match at the Myopia Hunt Club near Boston and a *New York Times* photographer on the scene asked to take my picture. He said he was doing a photo story on the most interesting spectators there. He took my picture and got out a stubby pencil to scribble down my name. When I told him who I was, he giggled nervously. He didn't quite believe me, as if he wanted proof, like a driver's license which, in Massachusetts, carries the picture of the holder. The *Times* didn't use the picture. Newspapers don't carry pictures of journalists, who are considered strictly background people. They are not celebrities.

There is no way Barbara Walters and I can compete on an equal basis. She wouldn't know this but she and I often have hustled the same story, the big, exclusive one that can lift a career to higher dimensions.

One story I wanted badly was a prison interview with Headmistress Jean Harris, allegedly the killer of Scarsdale diet author, Dr. Herman Tarnower. I wrote directly to Harris and received back from her a handwritten response. But everything had to be cleared by her lawyer, a man who gave approval and arranged the details.

I was away from my office when the call came from Harris's lawyer. My assistant, Quinnie McCray, talked to him. He was blatantly angry. He told McCray he wouldn't approve my interview because of a scandalous piece of gossip about Ms. Harris that had appeared in the *Boston Herald.* She repeated, again, that he was talking to the *Globe,* not the *Herald.* He said that made no difference, Boston was Boston. There was no mix-up with Barbara Walters's identity. She has visibility and it pays off. She is as big news as the newsmakers she interviews. She is glamorized by cosmetic geniuses and photographed by Francesco Scavullo, whose pictures of her have become slick national magazine covers. There is no way to rival that kind of fame power. Jean Harris knew who Walters was. Her lawyer knew who Walters was. Barbara Walters got the Harris interview.

Not all the fame is of the magnitude of Walters's celebrity. Fame can be major, minor, or anywhere in between. Whatever the degree, it can also be burdensome, unpredictable, and fickle. Yet the taste of fame can be addictive. You want *more,* so you try to climb higher, as if fame were a ladder. Then you find out there's no top rung, that fame is limitless, that it goes on forever and, if you don't know when to turn off your pursuit of it, fame can consume you.

Rod Steiger, who won a 1968 Oscar as Best Actor for the movie *In the Heat of the Night,* had a bypass heart operation in 1976. Six years later, when he was fifty-seven, we sat together to talk about fame, which he had but which didn't satisfy him. The desire for it put undue pressure on him, on his heart, on his marriage to Claire Bloom, which ended in divorce in 1969. He had been in analysis, soul searching, coming to grips with the reality that he was vulnerable, that fame is transient. He had mistakenly believed that fame promises a kind of invincibility, that once you reach a height, things come easily because you've paid your dues.

What Steiger discovered about fame is that it doesn't endure on its own. It is conditional and you have to sell yourself continuously. Steiger had ruined many lunches with friends by shattering the happy mood with a sobering question: "Have any of you worked as hard on your personal relationships as you did on your career?" None of his friends could ever answer yes. He became more and more convinced most people prefer exterior recognition, thinking that it will somehow insulate them from the ordinary ups and downs of life. He also likened the pursuit of fame to a fight in a ring, a pounding in a physical and spiritual situation where there can only be one champion and somebody has got to lose.

"Suppose you're a champion," he said, "who has fought fourteen rounds. The fifteenth round comes and you're being beaten. You can't breathe. You're a bloody pulp. One eye is already closed. Inside, you're hollering for your parents. You think you can't tolerate another blow. By some miracle, you reach out and your punch knocks your opponent out. The audience goes wild. You? You're glad it's over. You're glad you've survived. Then ... then they tell you its round sixteen. When you're a success, nobody ever tells you there's going to be a round sixteen.

"This really bothers me. I thought I did my fifteen

rounds real good . . . I thought I'd get to be a senior player, that there'd be no question that I'd play certain parts. I thought good work would be rewarded with other possibilities for good work. Now I'm finding out that this is a continuing competitive society."

The only way to survive the built-in insatiability of fame is to recognize when enough is enough. You can get avaricious about fame. That's when it can turn on you, when you end up working against your own best interests. When fame disappears or diminishes, usually due to circumstances beyond your control, you can suffer withdrawal symptoms. The trick is not to believe your own publicity. You must not be impressed with what you construe to be your own importance.

There is another down side of fame. Phyllis George Brown, wife of the Kentucky governor John Y. Brown, the Kentucky Fried Chicken millionaire and former Boston Celtics owner, found out that sometimes you are a prisoner of your fame, that it prevents you from doing "normal" things that other people do.

During her pregnancy, she gained sixty pounds. The birth was by Caesarian section. In her ninth month, looking fat and photographing even fatter, she hosted the Kentucky Derby. "Some people said I shouldn't go out in public and I said, 'That's phony and I will not let ego get in my way.'" Stories had been circulating in the press that her fatness was the result of a chocolate-cake mania.

"Why did I have to go through all this criticism just because I'm on television," she asked me over tea at the Carlyle Hotel in New York. "I was nine months' pregnant and I heard people say: 'Look how *fat* Phyllis is.' And, for heaven's sake, I was about to deliver a baby. If I put weight on, I am disciplined enough to take if off. Nobody has anything to pick on. My life seemed too good to be true, so certain people took shots." Priscilla Presley, widow of Elvis, once said the same thing to me in a single sentence: "When you're on top, people hope you'll fall."

Yet one of the great pluses of fame is that it is a form

of negotiation. Eleni Samios was a frail eighty-year-old widow
when I met her in Boston. She was en route to her home
in Geneva, Switzerland, and, through a third party, asked
to meet me. She was bursting with treasured memories,
life with a divorced man whom she went to live with when
she was twenty-one and he was forty-one. Open love relationships were frowned upon then, in 1924, a stigma that
could have resulted in social banishment. But her man had
celebrity.

He was Nikos Kazantzakis, brilliant author of *Zorba
the Greek,* and *Freedom or Death.* "Nobody shut the door
in my face," she whispered in English peppered with French
phrases. "I was accepted. It was because Kazantzakis was
an extraordinary man, a myth." She laughed softly and told
me they'd "showed a little arrogance," snubbing establishment standards of correct behavior, by living together. "But
it was a nice arrogance," she whispered. "We hurt nobody."
In 1956, a year before he died, Kazantzakis would receive
the World Peace Council Prize in Vienna.

But for years they were very poor, and they had terrible arguments about fame not being satisfying enough.
"He told me that freedom was not having to do what you
don't like to do," she said. She countered that fame ought
to bring with it creature comforts and she wanted that
badly, that when you are poor you are not free. "When I
complained," the old lady told me, "he told me I was *privileged.*

"He said: 'You are intellectual. You have a man who
adores you. You don't have to take orders from anyone.'

"But I said: 'We have no money.'

"He said: 'We have tea and bread.'

"I said: 'It's not enough.'

"He said: 'But we've also got olives and tomatoes and
we don't have to *obey* anybody.' Then he'd laugh and we'd
dance around the room together and I would forget.

"But there were times I was in a state of revolt. I would
say to him: 'I cannot stay with you without money.' Then

he'd pat me on the shoulder and say: 'Come on, let me tell you a story.' Every story he ever told me made me feel *free.*

"He had a great success in Greece. But it was not a money success. It was a success with the people. The government hated him. The church hated him. He was a man who told the truth. But he paid for his honesty by remaining poor.

"In Athens [1941–1945] there were groups who looked after famous authors. But not one of these groups gave us a penny. Kazantzakis was starving. There was a point where he couldn't get out of bed, he was so weak. I knew he would die. I knew I would die with him.

"So I went to George Papandreou. I told him Kazantzakis and I were dying from starvation. He got in touch with two rich people who sent us macaroni and sugar and a little money. And so we survived.

"Then, later, Kazantzakis got known in Europe. It was because of *Zorba.* Then the money started coming to us from all quarters. I cannot lie. I was happy with the money. Money brings with it comfort. We could never entertain because, being poor, all we had was potatoes and yogurt. We could never dress well. We were a little ashamed of that, but when the money came, the shame went."

Fame had finally paid off for Eleni, who married Kazantzakis, after they had lived together for eighteen years, in a Greek Orthodox ceremony. They wore wreaths on their heads, marched around a table as a robed priest read solemnly from a holy book. Friends even threw rose petals at them and Eleni discovered that love with or without formal ties is the same. What she wanted was love *and* the trappings of her man's fame. That was a long time coming.

Fame is a state of being that gives you admiration without involvement. It doesn't give you a real connection to anybody. It's safe and its nebulous. It doesn't hug you and kiss you and comfort you when you're sick. It doesn't call you on the telephone to see if you've eaten dinner on time when you're working late. It doesn't take you for a walk or sit on the floor with you looking at the family photo album.

When I pursued a career versus a personal life, I compensated. I've been compensating all my life. I wanted to do work that would be recognized as *valuable.* I thought that would make people think *I* was valuable because my work and I were one in the same. I was alienated and I assumed, wrongly, that professional recognition would cross over into my personal life, make a big difference in the way people saw me and how I felt about myself. I was mistaken. I married my career and proved my ability but, in the end, I have had to confront the reality that great chunks of my personal life are missing, pieces that cannot be retrieved. Time is the great enemy. It robs you. Barbara Walters was smart enough, and had the means, to adopt a daughter. She made a human connection, something fame does not give you.

But I was the one who set myself on a career course. No one forced me. Building by-line fame takes enormous emotional, as well as physical, energy. Emotion is not what fame gives you back. Sometimes, when you need admiration and encouragement the most, you discover fame is invisible. When you want to tie your whole existence into someone, when you want to interlock, you realize that fame is *something,* not *someone.*

How is it possible to verbalize to strangers staring at you in judgment, even envy, these complex feelings? How do I know they will understand, that I will not be misinterpreted? Fame makes people talk about you. I am not so secure, so confident, that I want to hear what they say. I would rather hide in a corner scribbling my stories, communicating from afar. I am afraid of fame. I want to be liked for my strengths, not disliked for my flaws. Fame makes no such promises.

◇

NINETEEN stories below, on the sidewalk in front of New York's posh Regency Hotel, chilled autograph hunters waited together in the November gray for Peter Fonda to emerge from his suite. It was ten o'clock in the morning and the fans didn't know that Peter Fonda, son of the then-ailing superstar Henry Fonda and Jane's brother, was sick with the flu, hidden in a darkened bedroom that had a faintly foul odor. Neither did I. Fonda, then a forty-one-year-old millionaire, an antiestablishment capitalist who wrote, produced, and starred in the fantastically successful movie, *Easy Rider,* which had grossed an estimated $100 million at the box office, was rich and famous in his own right. "My life has not been a total pile of shit," he'd say later to me and then make it sound as if it were.

Minutes earlier, I had zoomed up the elevator to his suite for a confirmed interview that had been planned to coincide with a Henry Fonda book, *Fonda: My Life,* as told to Howard Teichmann. It was 1981. The ailing Henry Fonda was flirting with death and his book publicist promised me an exclusive interview with Peter Fonda instead. When I was ushered into the living room of the suite, the female publicist blithely announced she had brought Teichmann there to talk to me, a last-minute interview substitute. Peter was "indisposed," she said, assuming I would be grateful for her trouble. I was appreciative, but not pleased. The difference in impact between a Peter Fonda interview and a Howard Teichmann interview is obvious. I wanted to know why Peter Fonda wasn't there. But he *was* there, the publicist said, behind closed doors, *sick.* Without thinking twice, I told her that's where I wanted to be, sitting next to his bed, talking to him. She was understandably furious. Later she would telephone my editors to complain about my unreasonable stubbornness. But while she was criticizing me, Mrs. Peter Fonda, an elfin sprite in tight jeans, Becky, interrupted to say she'd ask Peter if he'd see me as he was. She returned quickly with Peter's answer: "Yes." The publicist stomped off, more angry than ever. Teichmann exited in a gentlemanly way, one understanding writer bowing to another.

In the dark bedroom, Peter Fonda was laying off-center in a crumpled double bed, wrapped in white sheets like a mummy. Because he was sweating, he let the sheets slip away to cool himself and I could see that his bare, tanned shoulders were muscular, like a ballet dancer's. When he got suddenly cold, he pulled the sheets around him tightly, his slim hips and long legs silhouetted against the wrinkled sheets. His head, with neatly cut sandy hair, was pushed into a stack of down pillows. He kept his eyes closed most of the interview, speaking to me in a monotone hum, as if coolly appraising himself from a distance. It was easy to take notes because he spoke slowly, as if in a reverie. To my surprise, he began to confess to an identity crisis that had haunted him since his boyhood.

Often I have wondered if Peter Fonda had not been lying horizontally in a Freudian cocoon, half-dozing, would he have voiced his feelings about what it's really like to be the famous son of a famous man whose daughter was Jane Fonda. He told me that he was afraid that his fame wasn't all his. The reflected glory of his father's celebrity and his sister's celebrity blinded the sweetness of his own. His touching revelations about himself were interrupted only when his wife, who sat beside me, brought him a cup of tea which she stirred with her index finger. She made him sit up slightly to sip the tea because his mouth was dry. I thought I saw Fonda's eye open slightly in the pretext of sipping without spilling and, in that flash, he got his first look at the person to whom he was talking.

"Want to know what I say to Jane? 'Jane, don't worry. You know no one will ever call you Henry.' Well, I get called Henry all the time. Even after *Easy Rider.* I go to a party and the hostess says to someone, a guest, 'Come here, I want you to meet Henry Fonda. Oh, oh, I mean Peter.' So I say, 'Hey, that's not too bad. Never mind. My middle name is Henry.' People look at Jane as Henry Fonda's daughter.

"Jane, she was visible first. Before me. Oh, she'd done so well. Presented herself so interestingly . . . I walk across a stage, in a play, and I hear a guy say, 'The guy walks just like his father.' [Fonda shifts in bed, brings the sheet almost over his head, as if to block out what he's thinking.] 'Yeah, do you know what it is to hear that in the middle of a show? Oh, if they want to say it, let them . . .

"Ever hear the phrase 'third man on the match'? It's an army phrase. It's dark. A sniper waits. A soldier uses a match to light a cigarette. The sniper aims but it's dark again. A second soldier lights a cigarette. The sniper puts his finger on the trigger. But it's dark again. Then the third soldier lights a cigarette, and Jesus, he gets his head blown off. I'm the third man on the match. The target. All you have to do is look at the numbers. Henry. Jane. Peter. Yeah, third man on the match.

"No, no. I didn't try to commit suicide when I was eleven. I was ten. And it was an accident. I may be crazy, but I'm no fool. It was a single shot, an *accident*. I opened the breech of a gun, a pistol, to put in a new cartridge. Didn't hold it properly. The gun flipped around, the trigger mechanism was cocked and the damn thing just discharged.

"The bullet bounced off my rib cage, went through the tip of my liver, smacked through my kidneys. Did a lot of damage.

"When they told Jane, she prayed to God. Jane said to God that if He let me live, she'd never be mean to me again. Never! Then I got better. She was mean again. When I complained, she said that I had been a rotten little kid."

"When I was ten, eleven, or twelve, I read a book, *Call It Courage.* Can't remember the author. It was about a boy in the South Pacific. One day he went beyond the breaking waves to fish. A storm came up and he blows out to sea. But, God, he fights, he keeps the little craft up and he works his way to a distant island.

"Now, yeah, he's got to survive. He never grasped survival. But he survives. He fashions a canoe, somehow, and sails back. He is a man. Not in true years, no. He is a man in the sense that he has passed from insecurity to security.

"I lived in the shadow of this great legend and yet everybody was telling me to be my own man. A storm, and I came out of it smelling like a rose. I had to *crawl* out to be me.

"They found fault with me. They found fault with Henry Fonda's son. And I didn't understand why people would be jealous of me. But I was caught in a storm. An empty vortex. A lot of swirling, whirling and nothing to hold onto. I was caught by a powerful public surge to hold onto their chosen heroes. I was the son of a chosen hero. And I was still trying to find me. To find my way back. To the island."

Then he turned to me, suddenly realizing that everything he was saying was on the record. He raised his voice for the first time during the interview. "Am I making any sense? Goddamn, do you understand?"

MOTIVATION

IT WAS 1971. Two women had just been warned not to step across the threshold of the Ritz-Carlton Hotel dining room. The order was issued by a maitre d'hotel who was polite but resolute. The two women were dressed in pantsuits. They happened to be standing with their backs to a sign outlining the establishment hotel's current fashion rules. Female guests wearing trousers would automatically be kept from entering.

One woman, my hostess Marietta Schumacher, then-fashion director of the New York-based Roaman's chain, was being dismissed for wearing a Norman Norell couture pantsuit with a tunic top under her mink coat. I, having just returned from assignment in Spain, was wearing a Madrid-designed leather pantsuit by Mitzou, under a heavy, military-cut coat. We had planned a simple winter's day business luncheon. We had no idea Boston's Ritz had made its own rules about chic.

The maitre d', wearing a tuxedo at noon, something that has always struck me as hopelessly inappropriate, was not a vindictive man. If I agreed not to remove my coat at lunch and to roll up my trousers underneath the hemline of the coat, I could enter. As for Schumacher, she could go to the ladies room and remove her pants, which the maitre d' kindly offered to check with her coat. She could enter because her long tunic top could be mistaken for a mini dress.

Schumacher was wearing tights, a serious considera-tion in the interests of propriety. Being a sport, she decided to play along in this unexpected theatre, to see how much she could get away with. When she sat down, we discov-ered it wasn't much. So I ordered a small tablecloth for her to use as a lap covering. Imprisoned in my big, bulky, too-warm coat, I ate a cold lunch and devised a plan, a kind of hilarious retaliation, to get the rulings changed.

A few evenings later I went alone to the Ritz for dinner wearing a two-piece black lace evening outfit from the Avallon boutique, a Newbury Street salon in the Ritz neigh-borhood. The bottom was a pair of swishy pants, cut wide like culottes. The top was high necked and long sleeved. But it stopped just below the bosom, baring the midriff.

The same maitre d' was on duty. But he was so busy inspecting my nude middle, not a flagrant abuse of any Ritz rule and certainly more riveting than ordinary pantsuits, that he didn't notice that my bottoms were trousers. Care-fully I minced my steps, avoiding strides which would have given me away. He led me to my table where I dined alone, making more plans to write a column about this now-complete escapade of putting on the Ritz.

The day my story appeared in the *Globe,* the Ritz removed the sign. Later I heard that Gloria Steinem tried the Ritz's patience even further by attempting to enter the dining room in jeans, quite a long way from a Mitzou pant-suit. Gossip was that she was only allowed into the street-level cafe, an informal sidewalk room. For that stand of drawing the pantsuit line at no-jeans, I respect the Ritz's dress code. Steinem, a media child with a natural penchant for personal publicity, is famous for a wonderful exposé about posing as a Playboy bunny. If her entry in jeans had succeeded, she could have capitalized on a breakthrough that I had initiated months before. But the Ritz story got me a coveted 1972 UPI prize, and I have since seen hordes of elegantly pantsuited women enjoying Ritz dining, no questions asked except the choice of menu.

◇

STRIVINGS ARE based on risk. It's vital exercise, like stretching your spiritual muscles, seeing if you can get actual results for daring to stand up for what you believe. It may mean risking your reputation—the Ritz management could have laughed at my column, ignored it, and not removed the sign. The gamble is that you never know how things are going to turn out.

A dozen years earlier, I had taken the train to New York for an appointment with movie mogul Spyros Skouras. I was in my twenties. Skouras had big network television connections then and I went to his New York office to ask him to help me get a beginning job in television. He spent less than forty-five seconds with me. Skouras advised me to seek the services of a dermatologist, reminding me of a painful truth, that I had acne. Then he sputtered a thought that wouldn't have crossed my mind in a million years. If he arranged an on-camera test for me, which he quickly added he would not, and *if* I got a skin infection from wearing heavy theatrical makeup, maybe I would sue my employers which would, in turn, make him look bad. He said he was taking no chances on me. Skouras spiced his blunt rejection by buzzing his secretary in front of me, telling her to send in his next appointment. There was not even a polite good-bye.

On the train back to Boston, I felt small and insignificant. I came to grips with the Skouras rejection by telling myself that I had started the train ride with nothing and had returned with nothing. Therefore I lost nothing. When the odds against you are great, as mine were, you have to learn the art of patience. You have to wait for opportunities to occur, or manufacture your own, and, at the right moment, seize them. But it's the *waiting* part that hurts. When you strive toward something, you want instant gratification, like being hungry and eating well. Usually there is none. I had no contacts, no experience. All I really has was intention, but that's what kept my adrenalin pumping.

Seven years later when, by chance, I would be invited to do a series of television commentaries from New York and Europe, pieces that would be syndicated by Westinghouse Broadcasting to a half-dozen major American cities, I would begin to understand that a career is based on a certain amount of whimsy, like buying a lottery ticket. There is so much chance involved, so many unpredictables. Somebody likes you, sees your potential and wants you around. Or the chemistry is wrong, discordant. The only thing Skouras noticed about me were my pimples, which were soon cleared up with regular doses of antibiotics.

A man I had met briefly in an offhanded way at WBZ–TV, the Westinghouse outlet in Boston, saw me in a different light. Tom Houghton, virtually a stranger then, is the man who, in 1983, became senior editor of the Los Angeles-based "Entertainment Tonight," a syndicated show with a national audience estimated to be larger than the "Today Show". "CBS–TV Morning News," and "Good Morning America" combined. He telephoned me out of the blue. He said he was impressed with my *Globe* fashion commentaries, many of them page one stories, that they could be translated into television. How about doing some witty ninety-second commentaries for insertion into the then-expanded news programs beyond Boston? Calmly, he asked if I was interested. Calmly, as if this were nothing extraordinary, I said yes. Then I got on the telephone, asking my mother if she was sitting down because did I have a piece of good news.

My first audition was actually run as my first on-air commentary. Houghton proceeded to teach me "tricks"—

how to write short scripts that got to the point quickly, in tandem with the visuals. He showed me how to edit film. I had thought of sending Skouras a tape, a silly see-who's-got-the-last-laugh gesture, but he had died by then.

Sometimes you have to get nourishment from the art of striving itself, be happy with the reality that you're trying to accomplish some goal you've set for yourself. Purpose gives strivings momentum. The Westinghouse television experience was a part of a bigger striving which was and still is to self-maximize, to take what abilities I have and see how far I can go with them. Being taped for television by Houghton was icing on the cake, an unexpected approbation.

The real satisfaction came from pushing myself, stretching and reaching for this one thing, putting everything else aside. I was motivated by the idea of making my work *work*. I have always wondered if all successful people pay for their independence, but, in the end, somehow reach their goals with their independence still intact. The answer would come to me many years later.

$$\Diamond$$

BUDDY EBSEN was seventy-five years old when he came to see me, the white-haired, six-foot-four star of such television series as "Davy Crockett," "The Beverly Hillbillies," seen by an estimated audience of 35 million people, and "Barnaby Jones." But in 1938, at the height of a promising career as an MGM actor, Ebsen snubbed his boss, MGM movie czar Louis B. Mayer. His refusal to play the game cost him not only his MGM job but made him a Hollywood outcast for years.

The last talk Ebsen had with Mayer was burned so clearly in his memory that even after all those years he could recite it to me verbatim. We sat together in my living room one summer morning and Ebsen recited his conversation with Mayer as if it were a memorized script. Staring blankly, introspectively, he took the part, first of Mayer, then of himself, changing voices, switching facial expressions.

"He [Mayer] said to me: 'We're enthusiastic about your work. Don't turn your back on enthusiasm. We will give you the parts you desire. But we have to own you.' There was something about the word *own,*" Ebsen told me. "I couldn't stomach it. So I said to him: 'I'll tell you what a fool I am. Nobody can own me.' He said: 'Money is no object.' And I said: 'I can't be piece goods on your counter.' " Ebsen told me he was snotty, fresh, and that all he got back from Mayer was a cold stare and utter silence. "That was the end of me at MGM," he said.

Ebsen went to work as a vaudeville dancer, barely eking out a living. One night, after dancing in Scranton, Pennsylvania, he was driving his car over the Pocono Mountains to catch a train to Toronto to keep another engagement. But a bad sleet storm came up, his car had no heater, and the only article he had to scrape the windshield with was his comb.

"After I had stopped the tenth time to comb the ice off," he said, "I laughed uproariously. I said to myself: 'Louis B. Mayer ain't telling me what to do.' I was looking at myself from a distance. I saw the high comedy of a bad situation. This was something I couldn't control. But what I could control, being owned by Mayer, I controlled. Some men in this situation would commit suicide or take to drink. I laughed. I guess it's because I've always called my problems 'challenges.' I see hidden in every problem an opportunity."

$$\Diamond$$

WHEN I DID television, people would stop me on the street and say 'hello' as if they knew me. They didn't. What they recognized was the familiar screen image of me. I acknowledged that recognition, which gave me familiarity without ties. Anonymous friendship was comfortable because it was uninvolved, superficial human connection. Now, looking back, I can pinpoint exactly the memory that this feeling of distance was rooted in. I see myself at age thirteen, wanting to participate in life and being forced only to observe, a reality that hurt me then but, strangely, would stand me in good stead years later when I became a journalist.

I had been a bright high school sophomore, pretty, and wanting to be part of what seemed to be the choicest female group, the cheerleaders. At home I had asked to go to a cheerleading tryout and the request caused an unexpected ruckus. Cheerleading was equated with exhibitionist desires, the first hint of a leaning toward what was perceived to be an early form of adult male entertainment. Not only was cheerleading forbidden, I was banished from attending football games forever. That was my punishment.

One of the most painful memories I have is standing at a window facing the street that led directly to the football stadium just a few blocks away. I was peering out behind the drapes, overcome with a feeling of isolation as what seemed like the whole boisterous world was busing by, driving by, rushing by on foot, waving banners. I was watching a celebration of life. I wanted to be part of it, but I had been sidelined.

There was no place to go then but inside myself. Out of this feeling of being boxed, being set apart, I began to concentrate on what I heard and saw. Like a sponge, I absorbed the details of the crowd, snatches of conversation, impressions of the people and what they wore, how they moved. I had a secret notebook in those days and in it I scribbled impressionistic word pictures. Out of this forced introspection came my first love of writing—something I could do alone and in silence. It took me out of myself and it connected me to others, if only in words.

In some ways, I still am a loner. But journalism has bridged that gap for me. Now, when I interview, when I write, I consciously close the space between myself and the person I interview. That kind of instant friendship, though temporary, has given me the courage to practice being less guarded in personal encounters. In an ideal interview, two people carefully bounce feelings off each other, trading ideas, comparing experiences, weaving the tapestry of a tale *together*. Personal friendship is a lot like that kind of sharing, and I'm a lot better at it today because of my work. Readers became my friends, my audience, people I didn't know, people who didn't know me, but people who seemed to like me through my work. For a long time, I didn't face up to the fact that lots of people, even rich and famous ones, compensate for lost friendships, or voids of friendship, by looking for recognition from a lot of people they don't know. People in audiences. These are "safe" friendships.

I was astonished to hear Chuck Scarborough, age forty, a $500,000-a-year WNBC–TV newscaster, tell me a similar thing about his career. Scarborough, handsome in a blond all-American way, had married auto heiress Anne Ford Uzielli, and I had gone to their East Side duplex, a six-bedroom Park Avenue apartment, to do a story on the newlyweds. When Scarborough was launching his television career in Biloxi, Mississippi, at $1.85 an hour, Anne Ford was making her debut at the family estate in Grosse Point, Michigan, a bash which cost $250,000 and featured Ella Fitzgerald, in person. For his $1.85-an-hour, Scarborough appeared on the air and cleaned up the studio.

Scarborough told me that he came from an itinerant family, that his father worked for General Electric and that in eleven years they moved eight times to five different states. His first friendships were torn by the moves and, as he got older, he became guarded, less willing to allow friendships to deepen. As a child, he made a subconscious decision to protect himself from being hurt by future severed friendships.

"I suppose it seems like a contradiction that I'm in the public eye. I was introduced to broadcasting by my mother's second husband. He was an itinerant too, a man who went where there were radio jobs. The appeal of broadcasting was that it offered instantaneous social currency, a way to ascend the social ladder painlessly, without getting involved. People felt they knew you. But they didn't. Not really. They'd say hello on the street but you could keep them at arm's length. It was recognition without familiarity. Broadcasting continued my pattern of keeping my distance."

Scarborough was talking about the link between feeling insecure and using success as a balm for that insecurity. He was cut off from valued peer friendships because of his family's frequent moving. I was cut off from friendships never allowed to begin. Both of us had tried to substitute masses of invisible friends for one-to-one friendship. A lot of successful public people do that. Ostensibly I had gone to do a story on a marriage between a woman who inherited money and a man who made his fortune out of nothing. But Scarborough and I sat opposite each other in a child's room, a recently converted nursery for the youngest child from his first marriage, and we talked as if we, too, were children, comparing notes about motivation and inhibitions.

Scarborough and I leveled with each other from the start. I told him about my theories, that striving is the initial idea that you *can*, that motivation is the inner machinery of yourself, the thing that puts your ideas in motion—and gets you from where you are to where you want to be. He responded by telling me that he never made a parallel move, that he accepted jobs only to improve himself, to move up. That is the base of every striving, self improvement.

There's a reason I don't interview people on the street, à la Studs Turkel. I am fascinated by highly motivated *public* people like Chuck Scarborough who are empedestaled but human. It is the voyage to fame that sets them apart.

Motivated people go the extra mile because they feel they have so many inadequacies to overcome.

$$\Diamond$$

WHEN I WAS fourteen, I begged my mother to allow me to go to a Friday night high school dance at St. James Episcopal Church in Cambridge, where I played the piano regularly for Sunday school services. She agreed that I could go, but only for an hour. She would take me to church, pick me up and, together, we would tell my father that I was going to choir practice. It was all part of an elaborate plan—a mother-daughter conniving—not to make my father suspicious. He forbade me to go to such things as dances.

My mother made me a purple taffeta dress with a scalloped neckline and a sash. I wore it with a petticoat and black ballet shoes. I had chosen the pattern from a Simplicity catalogue at Sears. I had no idea how to dress for a dance. It was like going to a foreign country thinking you could speak the language and discovering that you could not. It was as if I had gotten there at last but discovered, once again, I was an outsider.

My concept of dressing came from the movies. Every Sunday my father rewarded my mother and me with two tickets to the one o'clock matinee. My role models were Joan Crawford, Elizabeth Taylor, Doris Day, and Lana Turner—at their fashionable best. The church dance was, to me, my social debut. I wanted to look pretty, the way movie stars looked. A big mistake. Everyone else came in skirts and sweaters, in bobby sox and loafers. Neither my mother nor I knew what teenagers wore to a dance. I had never been to one before.

It was one of the longest, most agonizing hours of my life. No one asked me to dance. I waited for my mother to pick me up, not daring to telephone her because my father was home and he might suspect something. I had wanted to stand out, not in a freakish party-dress way, but in a positive light. I wanted to taste popularity, find out what it felt like to be admired, to be in demand. But I never did. Not at a school dance, anyway.

In secret, with my mother as an ally, I had actually gone out into the world and joined in its normal activities for a few hours. I had great social expectations and the adventure failed because I felt *I* failed. At the other end of this nagging lack of self-assurance, highlighted by this incident, was the desire to succeed. For me, striving was based on the seesaw principle. I was there, on the down side, seemingly friendless, socially unacceptable. Success, the up side of the seesaw, would elevate me to all the things I really wanted, applause and, above all, admiration. I had not yet defined success. I did not realize then that real confidence comes from somewhere inside. It is not external. My desires were childish and primary. I didn't know then that what I really wanted was to communicate ideas, indeed that communication is the basis of friendship, one-to-one or en masse.

What made me strive to succeed then was the thought of praise. Money mattered much less than applause. Praise was not something I got much of in my life, even from my mother. Sometimes I begged openly for it, not in words, but by doing chores that would get her attention, like scrubbing the linoleum kitchen floor without her asking me. The only notice I got was a satisfied smile, a nod. But that was enough to get me to scrub often and well.

Many years later, in 1982, I interviewed Harriet Pilpel, superlawyer. She sits on-high, in a Fifth Avenue skyscraper overlooking Central Park. Her inner sanctum is the corner office of Weil, Gotshal & Manges, where she handles the literary projects of Billy Graham and Shere Hite, advises the estate of Edna Ferber (author of *Giant* and *Showboat*) and represents the heirs of composer Jerome Kern. Pilpel is a tough fighter, a grandmother who is considered one of the country's most formidable legal opponents. She has argued and won cases involving the reproductive rights of women.

Pilpel told me she once brought home a report card from Vassar that had four A's and one B-plus and that her mother asked why she didn't get all A's? "There were no compliments because my mother didn't want me to get what she called a 'swelled head.' On one hand, she expected achievement. On the other hand, she discouraged me from thinking achievement made me special. In a lot of ways, my thinking has been preconditioned by my mother."

Pilpel as a college student had tantrums at dinner. She was afraid she'd flunk exams and when her father would say, "Come to dinner," she'd get hysterical and say, "No, I don't want to eat." She added: "We'd soon be screaming and yelling at each other . . . I wanted to study, not eat. I wanted to study so I wouldn't fail. I was very nervous before exams. And I thought that showing confidence would be falling under my mother's injunction of getting a swelled head. So I calmed myself by becoming absorbed in my books. When I wanted to surmount emotional difficulties, I concentrated on my work. It was a great way to offset stress. I lose consciousness in work. . . ."

In sharp contrast to Pilpel's experience, and mine, is that of William Peter Blatty, author of *The Exorcist*, for which he reportedly got $20 million. Blatty is the son of Lebanese parents. But his father deserted the family when he was three, and his mother hawked quince jam on the sidewalks of New York. They were so poor they couldn't pay the rent, and every few months they were evicted. Blatty would come home and find what little furniture they had stacked on the sidewalk. But his mother imbued in him a motivation based on constant praise.

Blatty described it this way:

"My mother told me over and over again that I would be famous. I was the chosen one. Quite frankly, her attitude embarrassed me. I was ashamed and frightened. I knew I was not bright. And she was calling me *genius*. I was terrified that my mother and everyone else would find out the truth. So I handled the terror by knocking myself out. I had to be the first in everything.

"When I was trying for a scholarship to Georgetown University, I bought a book, *Thirty Days to a More Powerful Vocabulary*. The book was full of mature words. I worked every word I had learned into the essay part of the exam. My mother propelled me toward success by insisting it was in my future. I didn't want to let her down."

Once I asked my mother why I got so few compliments and she accused me of wanting everything "spelled out." I'm still that way. I need to hear good things about me because I grew up in an atmosphere that presumed I was unable to accomplish anything worthwhile. I want people to love me for the things I love about myself. When I advanced that argument to my mother, she countered that I had an imagination and maybe I should use it to assume people saw the best in me. She also told me I didn't love myself enough to be convincing, to show the world that I believed in myself.

At the time my mother spoke of "loving myself," I thought it was a ridiculous idea. Certainly it contradicted her Victorian concept of humility: "Be agreeable, be nice, no matter how you really feel." My mother was really talking about inscrutability, putting on an appearance of confidence regardless of being scared. Striving is strengthened by self-assurance, even if it's not real. She saw I was full of self-doubt, tense, afraid I wasn't smart enough, pretty enough, lucky enough to be all the things I wanted to be. She said that when you disguise your fears, you fool yourself as well as others. "This kind of make-believe could turn into a good habit," she said.

But my mother never voiced the idea that "self love" and "confidence" are interchangeable, that they are one in the same thing. The actress Polly Bergen, a trusted colleague, was the one who articulated that idea to me last year when, at age fifty-three, she married Jeff Endervelt, a businessman eleven years her junior. She was exuberant about that marriage and we sat together as friends, two women talking about the men in their lives. Bergen, a great professional success, confessed that one of her dearest strivings was to succeed as a wife. She had divorced theatrical agent Freddie Fields after twenty years of marriage. Bergen herself brought up the subject of self-love. It was something I really hadn't thought about in years. She told me self-love was missing in her life and it was probably one of the minuses of her first failed marriage. "I think," she said slowly, "it's truly impossible to love another person until you love yourself."

Polly Bergen had been in analysis for four years. Early in the therapy she started making lists of things she "hated" about herself, lists she brought to the therapy sessions. "Neck not long enough." "Legs not long enough." "Then," she said hastily, as if dismissing the subject, "I made a list of things I liked. That was a very short list."

Polly Bergen is a celebrity. Wherever she went, she was showered with legitimate compliments. She accepted them graciously, with a smile, and immediately suffered anxiety attacks. "I'd go into the bathroom, lock myself in and say to myself: *It's all lies. They don't really know the truth.*" The truth is that Polly Bergen didn't love herself. Her career strivings had succeeded but the image she had of herself was negative. She even told me that a "couple of times" she thought of "doing away" with herself because, as she put it, "there didn't seem to be a good reason to stick around."

Bergen is a southern Baptist from Knoxville, Tennessee, the first woman to sit on the board of directors of the Singer Company, the daughter of a woman who worked in a factory and whose father stayed home and did the cleaning and cooking because of an injured back. "All of us spend a lot of time talking to ourself about things we can and cannot do. We worry especially about our handicaps. Our age. Our weight. Our lack of education. Whatever. We spend so much time being judgmental about ourself, we cut ourself off from other people. When you finally come to terms with yourself, you learn to love yourself because you accept the things you can't do and change the things you can change."

We talked a lot that day about the difference between pursuing excellence and pursuing perfection. There's a huge gulf between the two. Excellence is enough of a goal. Wanting more than excellence is flirting with going over the edge of reality. You can make yourself miserable seeking something that doesn't exist. You don't find perfection in relationships or in jobs or in families. Once I asked my mother what she thought constituted happiness. She said it was having the good sense to be content with reaching a difficult goal and leaving it at that. A big danger to happiness, she warned, was always wanting more. She said there was an insatiability to strivings, that you had to know when to turn off your desires and accept the status quo.

Polly Bergen has no idea that she was reiterating the very things my mother had talked about to me. "In my heart, I always thought of myself as a failure. Everything had to be perfect. Of course I never was. If I did something in a mediocre way, I didn't do it all. I wouldn't play tennis because I would look like a fool on the courts. I wouldn't ski because I was not a great skier. Now I do all those things because I allow myself to be less than perfect. You don't have to be perfect to be okay."

I never really fully appreciated my mother's idea of contentment. I spent my life working toward what I once described to her as "having it all." She frowned at me when I said that, shook her head, said it was impossible to have it all, that no one ever really did, and asking for it would lead to eventual disappointment. I paid scant attention to her, insisting naively that "everything" was possible.

◇

WHEN Helen Gurley Brown, the stringbean-skinny editor of *Cosmopolitan,* first took over the magazine in 1965, she was scared. *Cosmo* then had 675,000 readers and was losing $5 million annually. The magazine now has a newsstand circulation of 3 million, which tells you that Brown is a supersuccess. But she grew up in Green Forest, Arkansas, poor, her mother widowed, her sister a wheelchair-bound cripple. Brown was a flat-chested ugly duckling with bad acne. There was no money for college but it was she who wrote the 1962 bestseller, *Sex and the Single Girl,* and became rich and famous. Brown wanted to write more bestsellers. But the *Cosmo* job presented itself. It was too good to turn down.

The first day she went to her office, forty people gathered around her desk. Every one of them was looking to her for guidance. She had never before been in a magazine office, never had a secretary.

"That night," she told me, "I went home. I went to my desk. What I mean is that I went *under* my desk. I was having a catatonic fit. I was in this insane grip of fear. I was immobilized, scared senseless. I didn't move. I had wrapped my arms around my knees and curled myself into a ball. I was not crying. I was simply paralyzed. My eyes were not closed. I just sat there staring, studying the wood on the underside on my desk. That's where my husband found me, under my desk. 'Oh come on, everything will be all right,' he said and coaxed me to my feet."

When Brown was sixty-years old, she sat on the pale beige sofa in my living room, a handsome brunette with a body hung carefully with elegant sportswear and fine jewelry. She had just finished writing a new best seller, *Having It All.* She was artfully made up. A chauffeured limousine waited for her outside my door. A female assistant hovered in her shadow, ready to follow commands. And here was Brown, relating an under-the-desk trauma and saying, with a sigh: "My middle name is struggle."

All her life Helen Gurley Brown has wanted to be

considered beautiful. "When I was growing up," she said, "a woman was admired for her physical self. I knew I would not be loved for my physical self." David Brown, her husband, is a Twentieth Century Fox producer, an attractive man who works in a place where beautiful women are the norm. *Cosmo,* which Brown heads, makes sexiness and beauty a synonymous subject. Brown, a stark realist, has spent her life working at being admired, if not for her personal beauty, for her astute appreciation and definition of beautiful things and beautiful people. To her, "having it all" means having a career that pays well in dollars and celebrity.

"Everyone needs playback. 'Pat me! Love me! Say I'm wonderful! It's one thing for a career to make you solvent. It's quite another to have it reward you with love. *It makes up for not being beautiful. It makes up for not being voluptuous.* Cheryl Tiegs and Farrah Fawcett just sit there and get loved," she continued, narrowing her idea of "having it all" into one specific, achieved goal. "Most people don't have that impact. So they've got to work at being a success in another way. I had a need, a yearning to have greater attention paid to me."

Each of us has a different dream, a personalized idea of what "having it all" means. But all strivers have one thing in common: the reality that there is no smooth ride to self-achievement, that the road to success is paved with detours, that you have to find a way to get past barriers or through them. Brown invented herself. She re-created *Cosmo.* She became a famous editor during a time when editors were considered "background" professionals who were meant to be heard rather than seen. Her strivings were based on breaking out of her own shell.

How did she cope with the down side of following her motivations? How did she keep going when there didn't seem a reason to continue? "Before you do anything," she said, "you have to ask yourself: 'Will this further my cause?' If the answer is yes, jump in with both feet. Doing it,

whatever 'it' is, can be horrible, dreadful, hateful. Maybe
you'd rather polish the silver. Sometimes you have to cut
through your own procrastinations. You may have to push
yourself, anesthetize yourself. You may feel desperate, the
way you do when a migraine headache is coming on. Well,
when you do it, all those doubts fall away. You are acting
on your decisions. You have to force yourself out of your
own pain."

Brown barreled on and I didn't stop her because she
made sense: "There are people who can't sort out what is
worthwhile and what isn't worthwhile. The dividing line
is a boring world called priorities. You have to put all your
major efforts into your major considerations."

She told me that she always took risks and that the
biggest was going to *Cosmo*. She was so scared she had
made a bad error in judgment that she became a frightened
heap hunched under her own desk. How did she get from
under the desk to behind it?

"For one month I let the *Cosmo* staff do what they
wanted with the magazine. I told them to do their thing
and I'd start doing mine the next issue. *The month was
like a survival period.* I was shrewd enough to know I
knew people who could help me develop my ideas. I was
frightened of what I was doing. But I didn't stop to think
whether or not anybody would read the magazine. I only
thought: 'I have to put out a magazine. I'm going to be the
best I can.' I thought that my struggle was worthwhile."

She also knew what it was like to be fired. The possibility of losing the *Cosmo* job didn't faze her because she
already knew what it felt like to lose jobs. In the forties
she was a secretary who dated a boss who was five feet
tall and wanted to have an affair with her. When she said
no he told her she had no job. In the early fifties she had
a job typing names onto vinyl cards and her boss, a woman,
simply didn't like her. "She fired me . . . I was thrown
out like the garbage," Brown said. "Maybe I wasn't as terrific as I should have been." A few years later, she worked

as a copywriter in an advertising agency. The account wasn't doing well and the three copywriters were reduced to two. "They said they could do without me."

Helen Gurley Brown becomes prolific when you ask a series of questions, one after the other, rather than one question. The more questions, the more ideas seem to pop into her head, as if you have set off a chain reaction. I asked her about her love life. Had she ever been rejected in romantic situations? Didn't "having it all" mean having a loving sexual relationship *and* having a successful career?

"When you face a struggle," she told me, "you pick up the pieces and go on. Even with all my mousiness, I knew I could go forward. The worst struggle is being in love with a Don Juan, someone who is not madly in love with you. That's a bigger experience. Emotional struggles are more challenging than work struggles. When you're fired, you get up, you put your clothes on, make appointments with employment agencies. Love struggles are something else. I've had the privilege of loving a Don Juan. I was with him for eight years. He was addicted to me because I could be depended upon to be very upset when he was having an affair with someone else. In that sense, I was reliable. I loved him. After I went into therapy, I found out I could love someone good as easily as I could love someone not so good."

$$\Diamond$$

NO CAREER IS without its pain and hardship. Helen Gurley Brown put it this way: "There's no such thing as being lucky every minute." The antidote to setbacks is to pick up and go on despite them.

Journalism is a job that assures no smooth ride anytime, anywhere. There is no way to forecast the outcome of an interview. There are too many variables. No two people are alike and therefore no two conversations are alike. The real journalist is drawn to these gambles, is consumed by a desire to acquire legitimate new information that appears out of reach. It's called "getting the story."

As a journalist, you can find yourself talking to fascinating people you would probably never have met if it were not for the job.

It is easy to be blinded by heady situations in which you find yourself. The truth is a journalist is always a journalist, never a socialite, which is exactly the way it should be. Sometimes it's easy to lose your objectivity. Yet stories don't just happen. You have to use all your antennae, all your charm, all your intelligence and all your wit to get what you want. Sometimes, in getting the story, you have to put aside brush-offs that wound the ego. You have to be happy that you got the story. Unlike Helen Gurley Brown, there is no great celebrity in a by-line except knowing that you somehow got an "exclusive."

$$\Diamond$$

IN THE WINTER of 1979 I was sent to Palm Beach to do a series on the inner goings-on of this real life fantasy island, a fabled place where millionaires reside in pastel cathedrals set in gardens that look like manicured tropical forests. One evening I was invited to a small dinner party of six in one of those magnificent stucco mansions. There I met a Greek God, Constantine Gratsos, a man in his late sixties, a startling Aristotle Onassis lookalike. The two could have been brothers, if not twins.

It turned out that Gratsos was indeed a major force in the $1 billion Onassis shipping empire. He was personally overseeing Onassis's magnificent Fifth Avenue Olympic Towers project. Gratsos and I talked informally, pleasantly. He told me that he was the surrogate father and adviser to Christina Onassis, then married to Soviet citizen, Sergei Kausov, husband number three. Gratsos understood the nature of my work, who I was and what I do. He was very open with me.

Out of this highbrow social situation came the chance to see Christina O. through the eyes of one of the men closest to her. Christina, who has a reported $100 million at her immediate disposal, hates the press. I had tried for an interview with her and had been turned down again and again. Of course I didn't tell Gratsos that. I simply asked questions.

Was Christina happy? "For Christina, happiness is the absence of unhappiness." Did Gratsos think the union would last? "Who knows," he replied, raising his eyebrows, shrugging his broad shoulders. What kind of a man was Kausov? "A gentleman. Kausov is sophisticated, very much so." Gratsos then proceeded to tell me he had visited the couple's Moscow apartment which wasn't the small, boxy, nondescript Russian set-up pictured in the American press. "It's big and new and quite elegant," Gratsos told me. "It can be compared to a very fine New York apartment." I asked Gratsos how this was pulled off. High elegance in Moscow? Gratsos revealed that the couple "cooperated" with the Russian government by making themselves visible briefly in Moscow from time to time. He was talking about the power of good publicity, getting one of the world's most famous capitalists, Christina Onassis, to feel at home in the communist world.

Gratsos even described Jackie Kennedy as Aristotle Onassis's "folly." Toward the end of his life, Aristotle Onassis had actually used that word to refer to Jackie, rather than her real name. "My folly," he would say, referring to his famous wife. Gratsos also confirmed that Onassis's great love was Maria Callas, that the two had spent much time together even when Onassis was married to Jackie Kennedy.

It was a lovely evening. Gratsos, a charming man, spoke frankly to me at the mansion and, later, at the restricted Everglades Club, which, ironically, had banned the Ken-

nedy family from membership because of their Catholicism. A week later, on a follow-up telephone call to Gratsos
in New York, at his office, he was a different man. He had
given me his business card in Palm Beach, his private number, and urged me to call him.

When I returned to Boston a week later, I telephoned
Gratsos to verify some of the information he had given me,
to remind him that what I had said when we first met in
Palm Beach about everything being on the record still held.
I leveled with him on the phone the way I leveled with
him in person. He knew I was a columnist doing a column—I even had taken notes in front of him on the insides
of several matchbook covers, something he found amusing
and original. He barked two thoughts into the receiver.
One, he had nothing more to say about Christina. Two, he
told me never to call him again. In Palm Beach, I was
someone who was an interesting social encounter, someone he met on more or less equal ground. In New York, I
was a journalist and he was an executive fending off an
undesirable, someone from the American press.

I took Gratsos rejection personally—how else can you
take that sort of rejection? We had clicked glasses, eaten
dinner side-by-side, even danced together. The job of journalist mixes as well with society as oil and water.

But the hurt didn't last long. In a broad sense, I felt
richer and far less confined than Gratsos. His world re-
volved around only the Onassis empire and its central characters to whom his life is dedicated. Every interview is an
automatic transfer to other senses, other places, other dimensions, other conversational intimacies. What soothed
my ego is the knowledge that I had unlimited access to
other worlds, that the Onassis story, although newsy and
valuable, was just another stop along the way. I had a
passport that could take me anywhere I dared to go. I did
not have to be socially registered.

My journeys always produced the unexpected. There
would be moments celebrities would invite me into their

environs, appear to the crux of a good story, and, in reality, promise more than they could deliver. And there would be times that I would meet people in offbeat situations and, despite their reputation of unreachability, they would prove to be quite open.

A journalist has to have a gambler's instinct, the willingness to take a risk to communicate. The payoff was always getting beyond these fringes to quotes that came from the heart. Risk, gambling on a story, produces either a winning or losing situation. When I got lucky with an interview, when people told me things never before told, I rolled with that luck, enjoying the winning streak. When I wasn't lucky, I turned my luck around, telling the reader the truth about what really happened in the interview. That gave the encounter the richness of honesty and proved that a journalist doesn't have anything to lose in the long run.

$$\diamondsuit$$

WHEN NANCY REAGAN was the wife of the California governor, I was invited to interview her in the beautiful but out-of-the-way Reagan home, a long and tricky drive from downtown Los Angeles. A secretary from the state's press bureau offered to drive me to the Reagan residence and she did. When we arrived, she asked Mrs. Reagan how I'd be getting back. She wanted to leave without leaving me stranded. The First Lady of California seemed angry that such a mundane question had been asked of her. Eyes flashing, she replied rat-a-tat that she had "no idea." Then she fell into a bored silence, hands folded in her lap, eyes glued at the lovely swimming pool sparkling in the late morning sunshine just beyond the glass doors where she sat.

Mrs. Reagan was cold, indifferent, inhospitable. She was not the perfect hostess. She didn't even offer to let me use her telephone to call a taxi. The secretary whispered that she'd wait for me and we returned together. In 1980, when Ronald Reagan was a presidental candidate, I interviewed her again, this time on my territory, in Massachusetts. I described her as "crisp, cool, controlled, cautious, and complex." When pressed with a question that wouldn't disappear, Mrs. Reagan answered a staccato yes or a no. When I asked her to tell me one way she had influenced her husband, she said: "I'm afraid I can't." She clammed up, folded her hands in her lap, and set her mouth in a determined repose. It was the exact pose of our first meeting in her California house. Nancy Reagan had not changed. She showed no signs that she recognized me, that she remembered a past encounter.

When Pat Nixon, with whom I once traveled cross-country from Washington to California, showed self-control, she was labeled "Plastic Pat." In person, Mrs. Nixon had enormous charm, was far less standoffish than Mrs. Reagan, and, in the middle of that lonely plane ride, slid suddenly into the empty seat next to me. She didn't freeze when I quickly reached for my notebook. I didn't pussyfoot around asking warm-up questions. I didn't know how long she'd sit with me and I got right to the point. I asked her about her "plasticity," about a legend of coolness that surrounded her in a negative shroud. She answered without flinching.

"I'm not afraid of anything," Mrs. Nixon told me. "Fear doesn't grip me. A long time ago I learned that if I worry about what might happen my energies are sapped. I balance the bad with *faith*. I try to see the best of everything—people, places, things. By blocking negatives, the positives focus more prominently. I get my strength from the people I meet," she asked. "When you communicate love, you get it back. It's a human response that is my energizer." I will always remember Pat Nixon as a singularly fine woman, guarded but not without heart.

The difference was that Mrs. Nixon had enough confidence in herself to feel she could *trust* me. Mrs. Reagan, perhaps more insecure than imagined, was taut and a bit pouty, someone who didn't seem to know how to play the part of a political candidate's wife. There didn't seem to me to be a Nancy, only *Mrs. Reagan,* in italics. She was openly suspicious of even the most innocuous questions. After Betty Ford became a recovered alcoholic, I arrived a few minutes too early for an interview with her at the Waldorf Towers in New York. The Secret Service cleared me quickly and I walked into the Ford suite to find the First Lady in the final throes of getting dressed. She asked me to zip up the back of her dress, which I did, and we talked openly, without inhibition, of all the anxieties involved in admitting drunkenness and conquering it. Rosalynn Carter, democratic in the true sense, invited me to a private White House party, not as a member of the press, but as a guest. When my mother died, she sent me a personal note. I asked Betty Ford and Rosalynn Carter tough questions and they gave me revealing answers.

Trust is one of the most difficult things to establish in an interview. Most celebrities are wary of the press. They love "good" publicity. They want to be empedestaled. If they are burned by one journalist, they tend to hate all journalists.

I neither write puff nor set out to destroy. I ask blunt questions. I don't coddle people I interview. But my questions usually aren't barbed; they are fair. That doesn't mean I don't seek the sensational. I do. What I'm after are the specifics of how people get from where they were to where they wanted to be. I want to know how they coped. These human strivings are more sensational to me than who's sleeping with whom or, as Rex Reed would say, the classic question that used to be asked of movie stars by Hollywood reporters: "Do you sleep in the nude?"

The greatest satisfaction for a journalist is not the money, which is important, but the prospect of sharing ideas on the art of living based on personal testimonies. Communication motivates me. When I am able to reach in and pull out of people these privacies, these feelings, when I can invade the psyche with the cooperation, the collaboration of the person I interview, I am happy. The joy of journalism is the communication itself, even if it comes back against you later.

When I interviewed the actress Jane Alexander, I asked her if she was jealous that Meryl Streep, her contemporary and a rival, had gotten more recognition from her screen roles? Streep, at that time, was on the current *Time* magazine cover. I asked her if she felt slighted. "Yes," she said at first hesitatingly, then vehemently, "*Yes!*" Later, when the interview appeared, Alexander didn't challenge any of the quotes but she wrote a testy letter to the *Globe* describing my piece as "sophomoric."

I have a strong sense of ego about my interviews. It's what I do best, where I have succeeded. There is only one way to get to the heart of an issue: to ask direct questions. My question asked only once of Jane Alexander was straightforward and honest. She gave me an honest answer. When she saw it in print, she was angry. I agree that there is something hauntingly permanent about the printed word. Once down, it is unerasable. During an interview, I take notes unobtrusively, keeping an accurate record of the best of the exchange. But the notes are often forgotten in the intensity of the conversation. And then they appear in print. Honesty in person and honesty in print are, to me, one and the same. To a celebrity like Jane Alexander, the gap is offensive.

Boston magazine later described that piece as a "finely drawn portrait of Jane Alexander as a capable, talented actress oppressed by the knowledge that she had not achieved the level of recognition as Meryl Streep." The magazine went on to say, "Perhaps the actress felt, uncomfortably, that Christy's portrait was all too correct; or perhaps she sensed that Christy was projecting her own feelings into the piece."

I had to smile at the statement. *Of course* I was projecting my own feelings. I do not come to the interview process a blank person, without emotions and experiences. It is from these feelings, the memories and responses they have evoked, that I ask questions. It isn't easy to admit to being passed over, underrecognized, especially if you've proven yourself and have talent. I have wrestled with that kind of hurt myself. To me, the question was natural. Anyone who works has felt at one time or another the awfulness of being ignored.

The irony is that Alexander's letter to the *Globe* and one I wrote to her, on private stationery and in longhand, crossed each other. I had sent her heartfelt congratulations because four days after my piece appeared, on September 15, 1981, she won a well-deserved Emmy for a supporting performance in "Playing for Time," a television movie in which she played the conductor of an orchestra in a concentration camp. But the *Globe* printed Alexander's letter. To this day, someone is sure to bring it up to me at unexpected moments and my journalistic ego winces.

There is no question that the egos of journalists are wrapped up in their work—not only in what they write about a person, but how they go about getting it. Ego definitely motivates my career—because of it I never want to lose a story. I am protective of interview time. I don't suffer interruptions lightly. When it comes to interviews, I am competitive, a fighter. Television celebrity David Susskind interrupted the beginning of an interview I was conducting with Ralph Blum, a 1954 Harvard graduate whose mentor was the late Margaret Mead. Blum had discovered an ancient do-it-yourself fortune-telling game which he called "Runes," had updated it, and, together we were studying the symbols. Susskind merely walked over to where we were sitting, his hands stuffed in the pockets of a fine navy pin-striped suit and, certain that he needed no introduction, included himself in the conversation.

Susskind, a man I had never before met in my life, showed me how he used his ego to get a story. While Blum was being photographed, a few feet away from us, he ran down his current achievements for me. They were formidable. He also blatantly mentioned his Harvard connection and the fact that *Globe* editor Tom Winship was a classmate. Blum had already told me his classmates were Sen. Edward Kennedy and author John Updike. Despite all the name dropping, the Harvard connection, I thought Susskind might make a good story if I could get to the real man hiding behind the credentials. I told Susskind to call me, that perhaps we could set up an interview.

His eyebrows shot up. He was offended. "I never call the press. The press calls *me.*" He called it his rule about journalists, as if he weren't one himself. I ignored the snootiness and rattled off my office telephone number. Susskind immediately reached into his breast pocket for a pad and pencil, quickly jotting the number down, pretending reluctance. He told me I was stubborn.

Men don't have that kind of tense exchange in professional situations. Business numbers are exchanged all the time, without question. Susskind reacted to me as a *woman* journalist, not a fellow journalist. He told me about his ex-wives, about a female executive producer on his staff for twenty-odd years, a woman he thought was a "virgin," although, he said, there had been nothing between them. When Susskind used the word *virgin,* he studied my expression carefully, hoping to detect embarrassment.

Then, turning to Blum, excluding me from my own interview, Susskind began to arrange a future interview of his own with Blum. They are deeply immersed in murmured conversation, a steady flow of questions and answers. I waited quietly a few feet away, assuming this interruption would soon end. Twenty minutes later I was still waiting. Susskind by now was joined by two business colleagues. The four men were talking in a circle on the sidewalk just outside the Boston Ritz-Carlton revolving door.

Finally, I interrupted the conference, saying in essence that Susskind had to get out of my interview. He turned to me and said, "Wait a minute." The men went back to talking.

Susskind was a competitive man who knew how to seize an opportunity. The trouble was that it was my opportunity he had seized. I have a strong sense of ego only when I am conducting a prearranged one-to-one interview, totally prepared, sure of my approach, satisfied that I am on solid ground. If I had Susskind's *chutzpah,* I would know how to play the *whole* game, handle trying situations like this with casual aplomb. True, I was irked that Susskind had pushed his way into my show. But I also admired his sheer nerve.

Maybe I keep my nerve in check because I know that pushy women are off-putting to men, that even men who claim to respect feminism are often offended by women who seem strong. With authority that was more manufactured than real, I managed to tell Susskind to butt out of my interview, that I was on deadline time. I even addressed myself to Blum, telling him: "Please come with me." In this extemporaneous situation, Susskind and I had competed professionally. Blum, in the center of the clash and on a tight schedule which included catching a plane to Los Angeles within the next hour, later observed: "You're just a vulnerable little girl disguised as an efficient journalist." He said it as if it were a compliment. But I didn't take it that way. If he was telling me I wasn't tough enough to fight for my story, he was wrong. I got it and it was a good one.

A week later, I pulled my car up to the sidewalk of the same Ritz-Carlton side door. It was the exact place where the Susskind confrontation had erupted. As I jumped out of the car and gave my keys to the doorman, Susskind suddenly jumped out of his car. Unknowingly, I had parked directly in front of his car, had actually blocked the parking space he was waiting for, a fact that he made clear to the doorman. "I want *that* space," he said, nodding to where

I had left my car. But I was a regular and the space that Susskind wanted was mine.

It was a lucky accident of timing, but Susskind thought I had deliberately edged him out with revenge in mind. Actually it was an amusing accident. This time it was he who thought *I* had *chutzpah*. He bent down and kissed my hand, the very hand that had written the Blum story. It was a princely gesture and I appreciated it. But what I appreciated more was the symbolism of the moment. Susskind and I were even-steven.

BEHIND
THE MYTH

GLORIA SWANSON was having a tantrum. She didn't speak. She spat out overenunciated words and raised her voice to high-pitched thunder. The roar made her seem stronger than the ninety-pound skeleton she was. The adrenalin gave the illusion that if she were goaded any more, she could inflict physical force. "Another question like that," she threatened, "and this conversation is over."

When Swanson, then eighty-one, uttered this declaration, she fixed her eyes on me and then deftly turned her head to the left, focusing on the front door, a stone's throw from where she sat, ramrod-straight. We were in her Fifth Avenue living room, adjacent to a crackling fireplace. It was early November, 1980.

My question, about the details of her newly exposed, year-long 1927 clandestine love affair with the late Joseph P. Kennedy, father of the late president, John F. Kennedy, was fair game, I thought. Swanson had just published her autobiography, *Swanson on Swanson.* The book would have been just another sizzling Hollywood memoir except that the most quoted section concerned an ardent liaison with the elder Kennedy. Swanson, nearing the end of her life, told how Kennedy, then a banker and Palm Beach millionaire with eight children and Rose at his side, fell madly in love with her. Swanson, who eventually had a string of six husbands, was twenty-six and married to the Marquis de la Falaise when she had her affair with Kennedy.

What I wanted from this interview was *more* than what was in the book. I wanted *her* feelings, *her* thoughts about the Kennedy reaction to her revelation, especially a letter from Mrs. Sargent Shriver, a Kennedy daughter who wrote that her father was a fine father, a letter read in part by Barbara Walters on television's "20/20." Gloria Swanson was in the news and I was doing an exclusive interview with her. Only she wasn't cooperating.

Gently I broached the subject of Kennedy again. I reminded her that the divulgence had made international headlines and that as a journalist I had to bring up the liaison because she did. She screamed back: *"But I'm fed up with this whole Kennedy thing."*

But was she *really?* She looked to me the classic egoist, a woman playing the role of the reluctant lover with studied canniness. The tantrum seemed to be a performance. Why was she staring down at a slew of newspaper clippings a male secretary had spread on the floor between her feet and mine? These clippings were meant to titillate me. She sensed my thoughts and said, more quietly, "I do not want this to turn into a sordid story."

There she was, a glamorous old woman who still carried a long-stemmed fresh carnation, her signature, someone who wanted to exit this life the way she lived it—sensationally. But Swanson was also dollars-and-cents wise. To give me direct one-to-one quotes on a hot subject would be like giving away something valuable that could be sold to any major magazine.

How to duel conversationally with such a woman? I studied Swanson: she had clasped her hands to her chest. Her blue eyes, purple with rage and fringed with glued-on black eyelashes, were wrathful. If I focused on the eyes alone, I would have probably fled. But I looked at her lips.

They were subtly upturned, like Mona Lisa's, and I thought
that maybe she was playing a game, laughing inside, wondering if she had intimidated me. I decided not to fight fire
with fire, but with flattery. I would display my knowledge
about Kennedy, but I would paint an incomplete picture
and, when her curiosity was piqued, subtly invite her to
fill in the details. I forced myself to be charming.

There had been an awkward silence between us and
I began to fill it with a recitation of the Kennedy chapters
which I had read and remembered well. I told her how I
had laughed when she described Kennedy as a bungling,
clumsy lover, how he once pushed her into the drawing
room of a train, bent over to kiss her and bumped his head.
When Kennedy straightened up, he had dropped his glasses.
Swanson admitted a tiny smile, but still stared straight ahead,
not at me. I continued.

I told her I was fascinated with her description of a
confrontation with William Cardinal O'Connell who had
tried to impress upon her the seriousness of Kennedy's
predicament with respect to Catholicism. I quoted the part
where Kennedy reminded her of his faithfulness to her,
pointing out that in 1927, "their year," there was no Kennedy baby with Rose.

As if delivering a monologue, I went on, telling her I
was particularly amused by her account of a European boat
trip that Kennedy connived, one in which he insisted she
bring her husband, the marquis, a trip that also included
Rose. Swanson admitted that Rose had flabbergasted her
by being *friendly* to her on that trip. She wondered,
then—was Rose Kennedy a fool or a saint?

The commentary calmed Swanson. It became a bridge
between us. Her shrinking anger was replaced by mild
interest. As I talked, she had assumed the gaze of introspection, as if I weren't there, except for my voice. Suddenly she snapped to attention and the mood changed to
anguish.

"Look," she said confidentially, "I didn't want to write

about him. I cleaned my bathroom many, many times to avoid writing this. But I wrote about him with dignity. I haven't seen Mrs. Shriver's letter. I haven't read it. I probably never will. Everyone has their own opinion about him. If they [the Kennedys] can live with that opinion, fine. I don't judge them, the Kennedys."

Swanson was beginning to respond. I had to keep the conversational door open, make sure she didn't slam it in my face. I asked a series of questions rapidly. One question standing alone would have been easy to dismiss. Many questions blurred together would make her think of answers, or snatches of answers, and that would hold her anger at bay. Did she ever come to grips with the fact that the Marquis de la Falaise grew tired of Kennedy's infatuation and this disenchantment led to her divorce? Did she feel badly when Kennedy returned to Rose? Did she worry now that her revelations might have hurt Rose, a sickly woman, when the book was released? Did she ever truly forgive the late Joseph Kennedy, a man who gave her a Mercedes limousine which she later discovered had been charged to her half of a business deal they shared?

The barrage of questions stopped her in her tracks. Staring straight ahead, still not making eye contact with me, she spoke openly. "That woman [Rose] is stalwart. She was a fabulous wife. Fabulous. And she is a fantastic mother." Then, unexpectedly, she laughed and said she had always followed her urges, whatever they were. "I'm not a sheep except maybe a black sheep," she told me. It was a wonderful quote from the "other woman."

Swanson, whom I had interviewed several times before, finally explained the reason for her bad interview behavior. It made my story. She told me she had lived in constant, harrowing fear of the battery of Kennedy lawyers. The name Kennedy was and is synonymous with power and prestige, and she was afraid to add anything more than what was written in the book, material that had been cleared by her lawyers after long and careful scrutiny. "For years and years," she admitted, "Kennedy and I were an item. People have been scandalizing for years. Especially during elections. People, certain people, would telephone me and ask me to talk about it. And I'd always tell them, 'No comment.' "

This was the big revelation, then, the fact that Kennedy's political opponents were looking to leak gossip about the Kennedy patriarch to the public at voting time, to swing the outcome of the election by shattering the integrity of the Kennedys. Gloria Swanson wanted me to understand that although the Kennedy romance soured, she was loyal to him in the sense that she never disclosed information to Kennedy enemies. That's where she had drawn the line. The book, she told me, was only her way of setting the record of the romance itself straight.

She was not a humorless woman. She told me that she, too, knew how difficult it was to get people to master the art of plain talk. "These days," she harrumphed grandly, "it's impossible for me to get straight answers to straight questions. I can't get the simplest information from my secretary. Like, did we call so-and-so? Did we give so-and-so the material . . . ?"

The interview ended pleasantly. Gloria Swanson gave me a copy of her book, with "Sorry" scribbled on the frontispiece. I went back to my office and wrote a piece: "Gloria Swanson: The Mystique." Shortly after it was printed, Swanson's male secretary, the one who had spread the Kennedy clippings between her feet and mine, called to say he liked my story best of all because it wasn't all "soft focus." It got behind the myth.

◇

GETTING BEHIND the facades of celebrities became easier for me once I understood the myths surrounding my own profession. Journalism is not a job that is associated with glamor except in the eye of the beholder. One of the main reasons I avoid parties, a habit that has earned me the reputation of being a loner, is that strangers accost me aggressively. The essence of the greeting is that, oh boy, do I have an Easy Street job.

A woman asked me, quite seriously, if a live-in maid served me breakfast in bed after ten o'clock. And was bed where I telephoned celebrities, directly in their homes, as if we were the best of friends, to more or less arrange a day of grand lunches and cocktail parties and dinners? It was such a silly impression of a journalist's life that it left me speechless, which, of course, the woman mistook for assent.

To most of the world, I am a by-line first, a person second. The real me is drowned somewhere under the ocean of words on which my career sails. I cannot go to a party and party. This is a big social liability. People assume, wrongly, that I am taking notes, mental or real. I am perceived to be a social spy, a strange character in party clothes relentlessly stalking stories. This is true only when I am on the job, which is often but not always. Once I was asked at a party if, perchance, I were wearing a hidden device similar to James Bond-inspired recording machines. People who have met me for the first time at parties have consciously or unconsciously moved away from me when the conversation graduated from small talk to important. My very presence is suspect.

At a formal dinner party at the Manhattan home of the widow of Oscar Hammerstein, the guests got to talking about pizza, favorite recipes and prized ingredients. A socially prominent New York businessman in a tuxedo had been reciting what went into the pizza he made in his own kitchen. Suddenly, as if a light bulb popped into his bald head, his eyes narrowed. In barely controlled panic he turned to me and said, "Don't quote me." I told him not to worry, but he did. All evening he avoided me, fearful I was tuning in to his conversations.

Journalism is serious business, a profession governed by standards and ethics. It has its fair share of kooks and weirdos. But it also has its heroes and heroines, people who see newspapering as a privilege not to be abused. I do not routinely bug parties.

Another common mistaken notion about the job of journalism is that to interview someone famous is to become that person's bosom pal. Journalists are outsiders, people who observe from the fringes. The famous do not automatically accept journalists into their lives, inviting them to step across the threshold of their tacky story factory, the newspaper, into their glossy world. Celebrities have post office boxes, unlisted telephone numbers, and a slew of paid agents who run interference between them and the press, acting as buffers.

There is a general notion that the press as a whole cannot be trusted, that they are dangerous manipulators, that they're "out to get you." Maybe that's true in some cases. But it's not true in all cases, and it's an assumption I fight constantly. I don't judge people by what I've read or heard about them. I judge them on how we react to each other, what we say and *how* we say it. I hope that's the way the people I interview react to me. Sometimes the chemistry is wrong. Every time I do an interview, I have to prove myself anew, test my abilities to handle negative encounters—and that's how many interviews end up. What looks like a cushy job is not.

Journalism is strenuous, demanding work with the incessant pressure of deadlines and tight scheduling that puts you at the mercy of the people you interview. You are also at the mercy of editors who have the final word about your work. Editors decide what day your piece will run, where on the page it will appear, and what illustrations will be used. Editors have editing privileges, which means they can alter at will, or whim, your story—with or without your approval.

Good editors are rare. Many are not fine writers but

they are the critics, the judges, the jury, and the executioners. When editors are good they are very good. When they are bad, they are horrid. Sometimes even fine editors can be picayune, as I discovered when I held an in-depth interview with Theodore Landsmark.

The interview took place in 1982, five years after a white man, carrying the American flag, used Landsmark for a target, wielding the steel shaft of the pole like a spear. There had been an antibusing demonstration at Boston's City Hall, something Landsmark didn't know about. He came around a corner and the demonstrators came around the same corner, suddenly face-to-face. In the span of twenty seconds, Landsmark, wearing a three-piece vested suit, went down in a scuffle, punctuated by a flurry of punches, kicks and jeers. Cries exploded: *"Nigger! There's a nigger! Kill him!"* It was an unprovoked beating.

A policeman offered to escort a wobbly Landsmark, his suit covered with blood, to an ambulance but he insisted on walking unaided. He was cool under fire, anesthetized by his own adrenalin. Even though bloodied, he reasoned that a published picture of a black man being led away by a white policeman would imply that he was being arrested. Landsmark's nose was broken. But let no man break his reputation.

It was very difficult to get Landsmark to agree to this first major interview since the incident. Maybe it was justified fear. Maybe he'd be targeted again, attacked. He thought silence was a necessary, prudent virtue. Reluctantly he agreed to the interview, but later toyed with the idea of not showing up. He appeared late, tense and nervous, looking at me suspiciously. Landsmark admitted he had occasional, deeply rooted urges for revenge, but that he was dogged by fears. He was wary of landmines, which could be anywhere. But he had tried to put this abuse in proper perspective. That was the story, a man making sense out of senselessness. The interview was emotional.

After I wrote the piece and it was scheduled for publication, Landsmark called to say he had second thoughts.
Wouldn't I promise to kill the story? I talked him out of
this reasoning that he, a blatant victim of racism, had a
lot to say to other blacks who experience prejudicial con-
frontations, physical and otherwise. He agreed, but not very
happily.

I took one final look at the story on the computer
screen and noticed that a copy editor had added, in the
lead prologue, the name of the *Herald* photographer, Stan-
ley Foreman, who had been on the scene and taken a
dramatic picture of Landsmark being beaten, a Pulitzer
Prize picture. Purposely I had written the lead simply, giving the dramatic details of the encounter and judged, perhaps wrongly, that adding the *Herald* credit bogged the
reader down, slowed the story. I asked a copy editor if
there was a *Globe* ruling about editorial credits for a competitive paper? There wasn't. I asked a second copy editor
if it was all right to remove the credit, to keep the simplicity
of the original sentence: "A photographer on the scene
clicked a Pulitzer Prize-winning picture." The copy editor
agreed. The original sentence was reinstated in the prologue.

After the story appeared, all hell broke loose, but not
from Landsmark. A vehement editorial in a neighborhood
Boston paper ran to the effect that the *Herald* credit was
deliberately eliminated by the *Globe.* My editor was criticized by her superior and I was called on the carpet. No
amount of explaining how this error had occurred was
accepted.

Columnists really never know what photographs will
be used with a story until it is printed. It's a little like
relinquishing your baby, your story, back to the hospital
after you've given birth to it, hoping it will be treated well.
I hadn't known it then, but the editors had not even used
the prize picture with my Landsmark story. There was no

important reason to give credit to that particular photographer in my story lead. When I pointed this out to the editor, I slipped more deeply in trouble.

What I found sobering about the whole incident was that my reportorial motive had been brevity, and what was being questioned were my personal principles. Every time I tried to explain myself, things got worse, like a picked-at sore that won't heal unless it's left alone. My editors focused all their attention on the technicality of a missing credit line and missed the big issue: that I had gotten a difficult man to talk about the details of being attacked because his skin was the wrong color. I apologized, taking full responsibility.

The world of legitimate newspapering is not always what it appears to be. Beneath the nobility of it, beyond the excitement of getting to the truth of a situation or a person, are petty squabbles and political attacks. Yet the human element of journalism, with all its imperfections and warts, is what gives it fire. Journalists develop an almost casual attitude of expecting the unexpected. It is the reality of their existence. I have lived my everyday life behind the myth of newspapering, in a dreary, windowless, computer-studded story factory full of bad smells. I have had to write amid the bedlam of ringing telephones and endless chatter. I have looked up from my notes to see men walking around with geiger counters, measuring the radiation in the air I was breathing. Three years ago I wore a heavy metal leg brace because of a broken knee cartilage. The doctor insisted, in the interests of mending the knee, that I sit all day with my leg elevated so the cartilage would meld together. The only such stool to be had at the *Globe* was an orange milk-bottle crate borrowed from the cafeteria. There was great excitement the day my assistant got her own telephone. But every time her phone rang and she wasn't there, I had to leave my writing and answer it myself. A push-button device was deemed an unnecessary expense by my editor.

Newspapering is an environment which, strangely, is training ground for the trooper psychology so necessary in getting an important story. If you can work intelligently in a newspaper office, you can work anywhere. It's a business that prepares you for the worst, which is just as well. Good stories don't fall into your lap.

$$\diamondsuit$$

I DIDN'T KNOW if it would be possible to have an intelligent conversation with Jeane Kirkpatrick, United States ambassador to the United Nations, while she was being whizzed to La Guardia Airport at the height of rush-hour traffic, flanked by two bodyguards and a male staffer. All of us squeezed into a chauffeured Cadillac, fighting the Manhattan traffic, veering this way and that, trying to get the ambassador to a pending White House party on time. The impression the ambassador gave to the press at that time was one of unapproachability, not the person you'd discuss nongovernmental matters with, a woman who was precise and tough in a military way. Even her walk was a march. The question in my mind was: Could I possibly cut through the image?

The promised interview, in the works for weeks, was to be one hour long. Yet, when I got there and had waited one hour, a UN aide calmly announced my allotted time had been reduced to ten minutes. *Ten minutes?* Yes, and during those ten minutes the ambassador would also be studying stacks of "highly classified" papers and signing the day's mail. In other words, she would be juggling the interview while doing several other things at the same time.

Ambassador Kirkpatrick was cool and reserved, as I expected. Indeed, she studied reports and answered my first few questions smartly, as if she had been blessed by God with the gift of double concentration. She seemed to be an intellectual superwoman, someone *Vogue* magazine had described as the most powerful woman in American government today. The ten minutes ended abruptly with a secretary entering the ambassador's inner sanctum, making several staccato announcements. The bodyguards were ready. The car was ready. The elevator was ready. It was time to go. I followed the ambassador, talking incessantly en route, trying to hold her interest: "Ambassador, you are a complex woman, a forthright woman, a woman who has shocked people with your frankness, your bluntness." She listened and laughed and said nothing. We were in the down elevator and I continued: "Ambassador, you are in the world of politics. No one really expects a politician to be frank, to be honest." No response. I kept going: "Ambassador, once you remarked you had no drive..."

Jeane Kirkpatrick, the woman who spent her honeymoon at a political science convention, the former Jeane Jordan of Duncan, Oklahoma, a woman with a Ph.D. in political science from Columbia University, looked stumped. She was making up her mind. The questions had been dangled before her like bait and she bit. Would I like to drive to the airport with her? She was as calm and collected in the auto as she was at her desk, deftly answering my questions, none of the men in the car saying a word. They had never heard their boss speak so intimately before.

"The demands this job makes on me, my life, are not amenable to a family life. I am in New York. My husband is not. We cannot meet, say, to go to a dinner party. This is a job I would not have taken if my sons weren't grown. No, I wouldn't have taken it if I had not been married twenty-six years. The long, strong, stable experience of marriage is necessary to withstand this kind of buffeting."

I asked her what made the marriage work so well?

Kirkpatrick didn't answer my question directly, preferring instead to back into it, to show, first, the absolute ridiculousness of society's evaluation of marriage.

"He is introduced as my husband, rather than I, his wife. Yet, on his passport, it specifies he has a dependent spouse." Her eyebrows shoot up in perplexed protest. "Now to answer the question. I never asked him to organize his life around my career, neither does he make demands on me. This is difficult, this job. The separation is really tough. The toughest thing on me is not to allow myself to feel unhappy. A month or so ago, I was feeling very unhappy. I wasn't even sure I liked this job. Then I weighed my unhappiness and I knew I was lonely for my family. Pure and simple, that was it. And, strangely, once I figured that out, it made me feel better, somehow.

"Emotionally, mothering was the most important thing in my life. It was emotionally absorbing, a total engagement. I am an existentialist and mothering was the ultimate identification, the real commitment. And it was intellectually satisfying, this watching human beings develop. Yes, yes, yes. I wanted a daughter. Very badly. It was one of the frustrations of my life, not having a daughter."

The machine called Jeane Kirkpatrick had spoken intimately, poignantly about the pull of career versus married love, the pain of having to remain implacably devoted to the job at times when she wanted her man. The silence in the car was deafening. None of the men seemed to be breathing. She had almost forced me to imagine her, the unyielding ambassador, as a happy, pregnant woman.

It was in this car, all of us squashed together, that I interviewed Kirkpatrick and scribbled notes as the car went around corners, streaked across the bridge, switched in and out of the speed lane. We zoomed into La Guardia, edged to the curve at the Eastern Airlines terminal. The spell was broken. The bodyguards hopped out, quickly opened the door for the ambassador. They gathered her luggage from the trunk and, in a huddle, disappeared together. It was a quick and natural exit, with only a split second left to say: "Thank you, ambassador!"

◇

THE TRUTH IS that, unlike Ambassador Kirkpatrick, most celebrities are usually insecure people you'd probably not want in your circle of friends. Gloria Swanson had, in fact, asked me sweetly, her voice like saccharine, if I carried a tape recorder. When she was assured I did not, she threw caution to the wind. I had no playback proof and she took advantage of that. In person celebrities can be taciturn, edgy, high-strung, moody. Jerry Lewis refused to allow my photographer to enter his hotel suite for a prearranged picture session. Lewis even tried to cancel on me when I called him on the hotel's house telephone to announce I was there, as planned, to do the interview.

"Forget it," Lewis said and hung up. I had a sinking feeling. But I gave him a few minutes to cool off. My instinct told me he might have second thoughts if I called back again.

Sure enough, the second time he acted as if nothing happened. Lewis invited me to come up to his suite. Of course the photographer was welcome. During the interview, he told me that he had been hounded by fans pretending to be press. He, too, had gambled that if I was "legit" (his word) I wouldn't be put off by his rude reception.

I was glad I didn't give up because it was in this interview that Jerry Lewis shared the details of putting a .38-caliber gun to the roof of his mouth, fully intending to blow his brains out. Lewis had been hooked for thirteen years on the addictive pain-killing drug, Percodan. At first, one pill was enough. By the time he was flirting with the idea of suicide, he needed one pill every hour. What stopped him from pulling the trigger was the distracting sound of one of his sons laughing in the distance. He stopped because he didn't want the laughter to stop.

Journalism is, to me, a labor of love—a long-term marriage of sorts. When I had a bad case of bronchitis, my doctor warned me that I was on the edge of pneumonia. He even threatened to call my editors to tell them how sick I was. But if I promised to go home, to take penicillin, to stay in bed . . . .

The very same day, a chance occurred to interview Lynda Johnson Robb, daughter of the late President Lyndon Johnson, and I immediately hopped a plane to Washington, feeling weak and refusing to look at myself in the mirror because I had a sickly gray pallor. The creative pull of journalism has often overpowered my practical senses. My story is my regular "fix." The challenge is to find new techniques to relate interpersonal conversations in Technicolor.

When I begin to voice these feelings to people, the strangers who talk to me at parties, the reaction is always more or less the same—"Yeah, yeah, so tell us about the glamor." No one believes there is none except, *except* in an ephemeral sense. Journalism gives you a voice, a point of view. It opens up the world and gives you vision. If you are innately curious, you see everything. A lot of people look but they don't see.

Lord Snowdon, the world-famous photographer, can't stand people who wear blinders or have tunnel vision. He wondered if *I* was someone like that, someone narrow-minded. He decided to test my sense of accuracy during the interview—his barometer of my worth as a journalist.

Snowdon and I were talking about having an "eye," the ability to see more than the obvious. Snowdon told me his late uncle, Oliver Messel, the famous set designer, taught him that "to see everything is everything." We were sitting together in his lovely Boston hotel suite and Snowdon, with whom I once had tea in Buckingham Palace when he was still married to Princess Margaret, suddenly reversed the interview. "Please," he said, "close your eyes and do not cheat." It was a facetious demand, but I did as he asked. Snowdon then hammered ten extemporaneous questions at me about colors, paintings, lamps, prints in the room. I got ten out of ten. Snowdon then asked a final question, one meant to trap me: "What's on the square table?" he asked. "The table is *round,*" I said, "and on it is a metal lamp." "That," Snowdon concluded, "is using your eyes." After that game, after I proved myself to him, he talked in a less guarded way. It is one thing to be a good listener, to make the person you're interviewing believe there's nothing more you'd rather be doing than having this talk. Seeing is equally important, part of the integral language of the story. Snowdon figured if I *saw* accurately, I'd quote accurately.

What balances quotes are absorbed impressions, observations of the nuances and details of the places and the person. It's what gives the reader a "you are there" vision of what really happened. Hollywood celebrities are especially surrounded by a myth of supreme elegance based on media hype. They are sold to the public as privileged, empedestaled, adored beings a world apart from the rest of us. That's why they're called *stars.* Stardom isn't always what it's cracked up to be. What you see is sometimes hard to believe.

$$\Diamond$$

IT WAS JUNE, 1972. The story contact, a Joan Crawford agent, was clearly embarrassed. He nudged me and said, in a very flustered way, that what we were seeing was proof that Joan Crawford had a "lot of gumption," a lot of what he called "social confidence." Crawford, Hollywood superstar, had shuffled into the hall of her chic New York apartment to greet us wearing a frumpy, too-big, zip-front shift. Her thinning reddish hair was in rollers. She had slipped her bare feet into cheap rubber thongs, the kind you buy at checkout counters in discount stores. She wore no makeup.

Could this really be the mysterious legend, the Academy Award-winning Joan Crawford, one of Hollywood's greatest actresses who created strong on-screen women, determined, assertive females with wide-shouldered clothes

and lips slashed in crimson? Was this the star who wore
Edith Head suits and Jean Louis gowns? When Crawford
left to take a telephone call, the agent cleared his throat
and repeated himself. The actress must believe in herself
"a hell of a lot," he said, to relinquish the glamor-queen
image.

It went deeper than that. The interview was conducted in a small living room in which all the furniture,
including the couch on which we were sitting, was covered
with great sheets of sticky, crackling, see-through plastic
to protect the upholstery from ordinary wear and tear. In
the middle of the room, on the rug, was a dog's bed covered
with towels borrowed permanently from a Holiday Inn.
This was not what you'd expect in the home of a star. The
Joan Crawford of forties and fifties movies, and the private
Joan Crawford I was seeing, were not the same. Sadly, she
had not gotten over the old insecurities of being poor, an
obscure Detroit chorus girl who, as a teenager, had worked
as a maid's assistant in a private school. She used stolen
towels. She kept her furniture covered and, she assumed,
clean. The contact read my thoughts accurately. "Joan
Crawford," he said, "is not without idiosyncrasies."

People hide behind walls, wear masks, lose themselves
in pretensions. It's the way celebrities hold interviewers
at arm's length, keep them at a distance. But the truth of
the person is the beauty of the person. To discover that
beauty is to penetrate the externalities, the barriers, with
sensitive probing. When this happens, there are tears in
the interview. Celebrities answering questions are shocked
to hear themselves voicing deep, unrehearsed feelings. At
the sound of their "real" selves talking, they cry. So do I,
both in empathy and gratification that I have shared a personal intimacy. When people cry together, it is a bonding.

There are people who shatter the myths surrounding
them of their own volition, as if the myths are make-believe
and therefore uncomfortable. What bothers them is the
illusion of myths, the assumption that they are protected

by some benign power who assures that they will live happily ever after. When people entrapped in myths tell the truth about their lives, they are suspect, looked upon as ingrates who don't appreciate the glory of being a legend.

Playboy magazine had featured Vikki LaMotta, a fifty-one-year-old grandmother, in its November, 1981 center-fold. None of the nude pictures were said to be retouched and they were fantastic. LaMotta was the second wife of Jake LaMotta, the 1949 middleweight champion who lost his title to Sugar Ray Robinson. The film, *Raging Bull,* starred Robert DeNiro as Jake, Cathy Moriarty as Vikki. She had come to Boston from Miami, where she lives, for this interview, bringing with her Christi, her thirty-year-old daughter.

At first Vikki LaMotta played the sexy *Playboy* subject, posing seductively for the *Globe* photographer, a showgirl with a spill of wavy strawberry hair, long nails, long lashes, long legs. She projected lustiness and she played it to the hilt, cocking her head sideways, gesticulating not with her hands but by lifting her shoulders and thrusting her breasts forward to punctuate certain words. She seemed blatantly physical, a mistress of body language. She had married LaMotta when she was sixteen.

The interview was coming along fine but I had no idea it would turn out to be terrific, that LaMotta would cry and I would have to control my own feelings to get the real story with a minimum of hysteria. It all started when I asked LaMotta about her marriage, and suddenly her shoulders stooped as if she were carrying a burden. The marriage was "good," she said, as long as she was "good." I was startled by her use of the word *good.* It seemed out of context with the interview, unless she meant "good in bed." It turned out that by *good* she meant obedient, sub-missive, docile. "When you're obedient," she said, "and I was an obedient child, you are rewarded. Everyone likes you. You don't get spanked. I didn't realize, until later, that they like you because you're doing what *they* want. I was ignorant. *Good,* but ignorant. Then I learned to say, 'Hey, wait a minute.' "

That's when her marital troubles began. Her husband, a revered fighter, interpreted her hesitation as possible rebellion, something to be stopped the only way he knew: with his fists. He started drinking heavily and reportedly resorted to violence to keep her in a state of frightened submission. I asked her what it felt like to be battered physically by the man you *love,* the father of your children? At this point, her daughter, a brunette Cher lookalike with long black hair, shifted nervously in her seat, her eyes widening in fear. This was not something Christi wanted to hear—the story of her father's brutality from her mother's fuschia lips—especially in front of a stranger. She certainly didn't want it printed. But Vikki LaMotta responded quickly with profound clarity.

"When a woman encounters violence," she said, "a terrible fear sets in. It is a fear beyond sweating, beyond screaming. There is a kind of shock. You are so frightened, you freeze. So frightened that you don't feel your body. You want to grab a hold of someone. But there's no one there."

And that's when tears streamed down Christi's cheeks, when Vikki LaMotta's eyes filled, when I could hardly contain mine. A straightforward question had produced an answer of a sad and dangerous reality, a strong man beating a beautiful, defenseless woman. Later, I learned this was the first time LaMotta's daughter had heard the story directly from her mother. It was a moving scene and the freedom of expressed emotion released LaMotta to shatter still other myths: Namely, that women caught in situations of marital violence will get sympathy and support from friends and relatives *if they're pretty.* Beauty can breed jealousy and the woman who has it is perceived as not needing outside help from anyone. All her life, LaMotta said, she never commiserated with anyone, never shared her deepest fears and hurts. No one ever took her seriously.

In fact, she said, those who envied her seemed "glad" she
was in trouble, as if she should be punished for looking
good.

Quickly, she asked me a rhetorical question: "Have
you ever felt sorry for someone who's pretty?" Never giving
me a chance to answer, she launched her own answer.
Beauty was as much of a burden as her husband's fame,
prizes considered so golden that misery was dismissed or
thought to be nothing more than a little inconvenience.
She needed help. Her husband needed help. But she was
a prisoner of her good looks. Her husband was a prisoner
of his celebrity. To the outside world, they had "everything." No one listened to her when she tried to tell friends
that nothing mattered except protecting yourself when you
were being beaten.

"It took me a long time to find myself as a person.
It's only now that I can tell you Jake LaMotta is good, that
I have forgiven him. He has realized he was wrong. He's a
man, just a man. Look, no one told me anything. They just
said: 'Hey, you're beautiful, you don't need help.' It's kind
of like that with Jake. Jake's personality is not likable. He's
abrupt. He's outspoken. He's not polite. No one is looking
to help him. No one wants to help a *champion."*

No one wanted to help Linda Lovelace either. No one
believed her claim that she, the porn star of *Deep Throat,*
had been forced to perform sexual aberrations by her first
husband and movie producer, Chuck Traynor. She made a
living playing a "bad" woman and that made people think
she herself was "bad." Then she launched a career doing
"bad" things on the porn screen. The evidence seemed
stacked against her. What she told me, in essence, is that
the image of badness surrounding her life had made people
assume either she lied or, if there was a semblance of truth
to her claim, she was getting what she deserved. Lovelace
faced a hostile world that believed good things should *not*
happen to bad people. *Deep Throat,* the pornographic movie
that made her famous, reportedly grossed $30 million. No

one seemed to believe her other claim that all she got was a total of $1,250 for starring in it.

I met Lovelace in February, 1980. I had expected someone glamorous like Vikki LaMotta, someone who'd project sassy sex appeal based on phony Fu Manchu fingernails, daring décolleté, and hairpieces piled high on her head. I thought her clothes would fit flagrantly, like wallpaper to the wall. I also assumed that her man would be dressed in equal flash, perhaps a suede suit the texture of churned butter and opened to reveal a hairy chest and gold chains. Yet the real Linda Lovelace I met was a plain Jane, an expectant mother with mousy brown hair that hung limply with untrimmed bangs that interfered with her prim granny glasses. She was wearing a drab, tent-shaped winter coat that wasn't wide enough to button across her bulge.

The man at her side was second husband Larry Marchiano, a $3.10-an-hour junkyard worker who said he had never seen *Deep Throat.* He made it clear that she was the woman he loved, that he cared nothing for her past. Lovelace was six months pregnant with her second child from Marchiano, a man whose old, faded sportswear had the tattered look of too many machine washings. I asked her why she had been drawn to Marchiano, a simple man so different from her first husband and manager, Chuck Traynor, a man who drove a wine-colored Jaguar and talked about sky diving. "Because he is *normal,*" she said about Marchiano and repeated the one key word in the sentence: *"Normal!"* Neither looked comfortable in the Ritz-Carlton, where the interview was being conducted, but she smiled wanly when he held her hand. She was meeting the press because she claimed that Traynor, who had denied everything, had made her his prisoner for two years, forced her into horrible sex perversions, never let her out of his sight, even when she went to the bathroom. *"He came with me,"* she insisted during my interview. *"He stood right there."* I found this hard to believe, especially if they were in a public place, say a restaurant. I told her so.

When she asked to be excused, to go to a public ladies room, what did Traynor do? "I was not allowed unless the ladies room had no windows." How would Traynor possibly know that? "He only took me to restaurants where he knew exactly what the ladies rooms looked like." At press conferences, Lovelace had told reporters she was a natural exhibitionist and I reminded her of that. She told me her comments were painstakingly rehearsed, that she was coached by Traynor, brainwashed. She had to say "convincingly" what she had been told to say or Traynor beat her badly. Lovelace told me she plotted her escape from him by making excuses to leave him first for a minute or two, then for ten minutes at a time. "And I put on a wig and dark glasses and lay down on the floor of a friend's automobile and got away."

The tears started when her mother entered the conversation. Lovelace, an expectant mother, choked on the word, sobbed, wiping away the tears with her bare hands. She didn't even have a tissue.

Hers were not crocodile tears. She told me her mother used buckle belts, ropes, and mop handles to beat her. Once her father, a retired Miami policeman who turned away from the beatings, had to "pull her [her mother] off from me." "I was not Miss Holy Holy," she said simply, explaining that at age twenty she gave birth to an illegitimate child. Then, in a whisper that was hard to hear, she asked me a question which has always haunted me: "Why didn't somebody do something?" And she cried some more.

$$\Diamond$$

STEP INTO the world of journalism and you are hit by an avalanche of daily battles which are part of the run, battles you've got to love to win. The fight to get the celebrity first, *fast.* The fight to coax, prod, cajole illuminating quotes. The fight to meet deadlines. Even after all the immediate fights are won, there is the ever-present challenge for sustained excellence. It looms like a flashing neon sign, goading you not to get too comfortable or you'll find yourself in a rut. Success in journalism is temporary, just as a newspaper is disposable. Yesterday's story is gone, forgotten. The urgency of newspapering is hammered home anew each and every time I interview someone.

Perish the thought that a journalist merely scribbles whatever nonsense a celebrity utters. That's not how good stories happen. The journalist must be wary of canned chitchat, memorized comments celebrities repeat, usually out of laziness or boredom. I *also* memorize key comments that celebrities have said in other interviews, things I've studied carefully in library files, and when they surface, when I say "Yes, I read that in an interview where you also said . . ." the celebrity involved is usually embarrassed at being "found out," surprised that a journalist has done homework. The fluster gives me a psychological edge, and I use it. The split second the interviewee is wondering if he or she "slipped" in my eyes, I bait other questions— knowing that the person's guard is down at that moment. That is one way I've gotten some of my best quotes. My questions are geared to get as close as possible to a line of feelings that have produced action in that person's life. I probe what makes people do things, react in a particular way. These are what make them visible to the reader. The trick, if you can call it that, is to make the interview and story seem effortless. But the truth is that a lot of effort goes into what appears to be effortlessness.

Some journalists are wined and dined nonstop. "Suzy," or Aileen Mehle of the *New York Daily News,* is one of the most sought-after, coddled society columnists in New York. She looks like a Hollywood starlet, with great coifs of vanilla ringlets spilling helter-skelter around bare shoulders and melting into low necklines. She *is* glamorous. But I saw her once at the midnight supper at a millionaire's New York townhouse, standing near the door, watching who was entering and exiting with whom. She was taking notes on a miniscule Gucci pad. She could not go to a party and party as well. She was wearing a dark business suit. The glamorous photos of her in slick magazines were just part of a frothy glamor image. Suzy hardly spoke to me that night. When we were introduced, she nodded. That was it. There was no time to be charming. She was *working*.

Then there are the bullying journalists, the "60 Minutes" crew who interrogate rather than interview. Sometimes they use the technique of summarizing statements they want to elicit and cannot, the impact of a compendium reflected in a close-up of the pained facial expression. This is vinegar journalism, cutthroat, tough, and enormously effective. Mike Wallace explained his interview techniques to me this way: "You set out to do an interview and you do it the way you have to do it." He meant there are no holds barred.

Sitting at lunch with Mike Wallace, I had asked what I thought was an innocuous question, one of those typical warm-up questions he might use to relax interviewees: How does he decide who he's going to interview?

Wallace bristled. He didn't answer directly. I goaded him by taking the question a step further. Did he deliberately choose people in the searing eye of controversy and thus escalate the controversy? "Don't push me," he snapped. "Let me figure this out for myself." He was stalling. Wallace's smile became only a fraction of a smile, like a television tape put on hold.

"This is difficult," he said. "I've never really defined that for myself." He was hedging. Here was a man who held questions to people like knives, but squirmed when he himself had to answer a simple one. An interviewer who does not like being interviewed.

Wallace didn't try to escape me but he used humor to get himself off the hook. "Now Myron," he said using his real name, "you've got to have an answer to this." But he never did. This was the Mike Wallace whose questions have been compared to hammer blows, a man whose salary is well into the six figures, a man who is a brilliant adversary interviewer. I asked him why he was so rough on interviewees. "I like to succeed," he told me. "I'm in a competitive profession."

Wallace, the son of Russian immigrants, reminded me he was from New England, that the Puritan work ethic was in his blood. He emphasized that hard work alone was the key to his success. I reminded him that the work ethic isn't regional, that television news is legendary for its cutthroat image, that rivalry in the interview game is tantamount to being in shark infested waters.

"Don't be asinine," he retorted. "That's an asinine assumption. All you have to do is be prepared." But at another point in the interview, Dan Rather's name popped up. And what Wallace said about Rather contradicted his previous portrait of television not being competitive. "That man," he said, referring to Rather, "treats me kindly. I'm not used to that among competitors. No," he suddenly corrected himself, "I don't mean competitors, I mean colleagues." His smile reflected embarrassment at the slipped truth.

"You know," he finally admitted, *"that all reporters are turf jealous."*

And that is the unadulterated truth. Journalists are secretly jealous of each other. They pretend camaraderie, but it's not true. They're scared of each other. They're always watching each other, comparing each other's work. And why not? They're in a race. There's an inherent immediacy to the race. News is *timely* and it's easy to get passed by and over if you don't push. The whole news organization has to push and then shove. That's often what happens in the interview process itself.

The syndicated television show, "Entertainment Tonight," ran an insightful piece on the three network behind-the-scenes persons who booked celebrities for morning news shows. Each person revealed a desperate clawing, a we'll-go-to-any-lengths attitude to get a celebrity exclusively. Once the celebrity is on the air, the point of the exercise is for the interviewer to get him or her to say things he or she have never said before. The same is true for print journalists.

Wallace couldn't help but point out that this interview began with small talk about the swan boats in the Boston Public Garden. "You," he said, "hammered home questions and I don't find you a sharkess."

Journalistic toughness takes many forms. Sometimes it can be just hanging in there when an interview seems impossible. The toughness may be a gut, split-second decision on how to approach an interviewee who doesn't really want to be interviewed except superfluously. Sometimes it's simply displaying the courage to approach an interview as yourself, without pretensions. You don't have to *act* the role of journalist. You concentrate so completely on the job at hand that you lose yourself in the exchange. This is the hardest method, but produces the best results.

You cannot peel away anybody else's veneer unless you, too, dare to come to the interview as you are. But Mike Wallace's advice about being prepared is vital. You have to know exactly what you want from an interview and then you have to wing it because there are so many unpredictables.

◇

WHEN CYRUS VANCE was Jimmy Carter's secretary of state, he made himself inaccessible to me for what was termed "the time being." That meant I was being put on hold indefinitely. When Vance clashed with Zbigniew Brzezinski, Carter's national security adviser, and then tangled with Andrew Young, the ambassador to the United Nations, I tried again. Vance's spokesperson made it clear that an interview with Cyrus Vance was out of the question. Vance came through as intellectual statesman too busy to talk to the press.

Vance, like many celebrities, made himself available to me only when he, a liberal Democrat and New York lawyer, published a book, *Hard Choices*, in June, 1983. Vance had resigned from the Carter cabinet in 1980, when Carter made the decision to attempt military rescue of the American hostages in Iran. Carter did not consult Vance, who was insulted at being ignored. Now the only reason Vance agreed to see me was to hype his book. I grabbed the token interview, hoping to distract him from quoting from his book. Author interviews are opportunities to turn an interview situation around. Could I really get this public man to reflect private feelings? I wanted to know how he felt when Carter, his boss and supposed friend, announced to the world that Edmund Muskie, who followed Vance, was a more "evocative" secretary of state? How did it feel to be betrayed by someone you had trusted? Someone who happened to be the president of the United States? I had read somewhere that Vance was greatly influenced by his mother, a young widow. Could I pry out of him his private relationship with her?

Much to my surprise, Vance arranged a luncheon interview for *three*, bringing his wife, the former Grace Sloane, who came wearing a pink Ultrasuede suit. Clearly, she was there to audit the interview. Highly placed professional men don't bring their wives to press interviews. They are usually accompanied by sophisticated public relations spokespersons who sit silently, observing, listening but never interrupting. The best public relations people are like flies on the wall. You forget their presence. Obviously Mrs. Vance was present to protect her husband from anticipated hostile questions with nods and eye signals to approve answers, approaches, reactions.

The challenge was thus not only to reach Cyrus Vance, it was to reach him by getting around Mrs. Cyrus Vance, an unexpected complication. Obviously this was a close-knit husband-and-wife team sitting opposite each other. I, the third party, was sandwiched between them. These two people knew each other's secrets, and now I had to deal with two minds, two spirits acting as one. I thought of it as double jeopardy.

Cyrus Vance is a gangly, Yale-educated barrister called Spider by friends because he seems to be all arms and legs. To me, he looked like an intellectual Howdy Doody in a business suit. I had to decide quickly how to approach the man in front of his wife. I had not read Vance's book. I told him so. It had, in fact, arrived in my office only an hour or two before the interview. But I had researched him well in the *Globe* library and had come away with one overriding impression: Cyrus Vance had the courage of his convictions. He bent for no one, including Jimmy Carter. Although he was a professional negotiator, he didn't compromise on important principles. He wrote his resignation to Carter in longhand and delivered it personally.

I told Vance that I wanted to talk about the connection between courage and power. His eyebrows shot up in surprise, his only reaction. There was silence between us. Vance looked to his wife for approval and she nodded slightly to him. Then he gazed at me with renewed interest, as if challenging me to keep his interest level buoyed. I generalized the subject—courage—coasting with it, leaving it open so he could take it where he wanted. Then I'd decide if the direction worked, keeping him on track. I wanted him to think he had the lead.

Vance is an erudite man. He went to the Kent School in Connecticut, graduated from Yale in 1939, then obtained a law degree with honors in 1942 from Yale Law School. He had been general counsel to the Pentagon. He was Kennedy's secretary of the army and Johnson's deputy secretary of defense. I knew I'd have to ask Vance direct questions but with the twist of originality, questions that would somehow address the heart and spirit as well as the mind.

The moment Vance saw me open my notebook and poise my pencil, he cleared his throat and, as if on cue, began talking rapidly, stuffily about diplomacy, as if dictating a boring speech. Interviews have a body language.

I did not move my pencil, a gesture meant to make him understand that he was not on the right track. Vance got the message. I wanted the interview to be the result of two intelligences, his and mine. He stopped talking and I started.

He had come to the interview wearing a facade. Vance assumed this encounter was nothing more than a polite public relations function. He did not imagine that the interview could become interpersonal. But I did. Carefully I phrased questions geared to make him think more like a man than a man of power. This was one time I used a soft-core version of the hard-core Mike Wallace approach. I asked a series of direct questions, not any that would nail him hard, and Cyrus Vance answered from the heart rather than the head. I knew I had gotten the story, the vision of an ordinary man at an extraordinarily rarefied power level.

Vance and I played "conversation" as if it were a fast-passed tennis game with no fumbles. The ball soared back and forth across the net which, in reality, was a small round table with a pink tablecloth and flowers.

Did he ever feel guilty about the headiness of his power? "A lot of people don't believe I shrink from the use of power," he said. "But I know this about power: You don't stick your finger in somebody's eye just to prove you're powerful. You don't go around picking fights."

What influence did his mother have on his approach to international negotiating? "When I was six or seven, my mother told me not to do something. I edged across the line of demarcation. When she asked me about this, I gave her an equivocal answer. She said she understood I had not lied, exactly, but she made it clear that being an equivocator is not tolerable."

Do you make mistakes? "I like a decent night's sleep. Every day when I get up, I like to think what lies ahead. At night, before I go to bed, I evaluate the day, I like to think I did the best I can. But if I've made a mistake, I learn from it. Actually, I've made many mistakes . . . and I don't make the same mistake twice."

What does it feel like to be criticized publicly? "If the criticism is nasty, you get angry. I blow up for a while. Then I go on to something else. People who dwell on their anger find that anger clouds their thinking. Anger saps your energy."

Is Jimmy Carter an ex-friend? "I was hurt by the things he said when I left office. He was critical of me . . . that hurt. But even those feelings have faded. It was the reaction of an individual who was mad I had left him. So I forgave him."

What about Brzezinski with whom he had sparred? "I do not intend to get into a personal mud-slinging contest with Brzezinski. I do not think the differences should be personalized. Personalized differences get you nowhere."

$$\Diamond$$

THE FAMILY PHOTO album has a picture of me I've never liked. It was taken by my mother in the backyard of our house on the first day of my sophomore year in high school. Smiling, yes. But it was a fake smile. A big cover-up. New clothes. But they were too big, especially the long red plaid skirt. It was held at the waist by a big safety pin. That made the waistline smaller but lumpy, bunched-up fabric threw my left hip out of kilter. A biggish white sweater concealed the situation, barely.

There was no money for a continuous wardrobe. That's why that picture was taken, a permanent record of having had new clothes that one special time. In those days, clothes had to last indefinitely. You were supposed to "grow" into them, even at fifteen. Each purchase, spaced far apart in time, was purposely chosen two sizes too big. The trouble was I grew taller, not sideways. I felt small in those big clothes.

When I look at that picture, I look right through it to

the place inside me where all my insecurities lie dormant, until something happens to make me feel smaller than I really am. Then, just like in the picture, I stand tall, smile a bit, appear secure. But, again, it's a cover-up. Even in those days I felt different, but the differentness went deeper than the clothes. It was something that worked itself from the inside out and I kept it just below the surface of me. The largeness of what I was wearing just seemed to punctuate that differentness. In that picture I still see the lingering pain of feeling like a misfit.

But I have showed that picture to friends and no one noticed the size of my clothes. Maybe it was because I purposely stood at an angle so that the frumpy part of me was half-hidden. I had figured out a way to disguise my insecurity.

Insecurity is something I've spent my whole life trying to overcome. But there's a good side to insecurity. It gives you the momentum of motivation. I was not contented with that picture of me. That was not the way I wanted to look to others, how I wanted to see myself. I wanted self-harmony, a feeling of easiness with my image. I wanted my clothes to fit me and my lifestyle. I wanted this badly, not casually. Journalism has made that possible for me. But it took me a long time to find that out about myself, to discover that I am a fighter. When that picture was taken, I didn't know any of this about my potential, I only felt painfully insecure about myself.

That very week, my mother and I visited an austere aunt, one of my father's more forbidding sisters, a rich woman with an adopted daughter my age. The aunt was in the process of mailing a large bundle of used clothing somewhere. There, like a mirage, on the top of the bundle was a red plaid skirt, my *real* size. I begged this aunt, now dead, not to mail it away, but to give it to me. I even tried it on, showing her how well it fit. Her gesture was cruel and final. She took the skirt from my hands, folded it back in the box and closed the lid. I was too young, too impressionable, too silly to reason that maybe someone else needed that skirt more than I did.

Even now, despite all my success, I am still trying to realize the full measure of my own worth. Now I know my own weaknesses and that has added immeasurably to my strength. In the beginning, I allowed little hurts to become big issues. I thought I wasn't pretty enough, smart enough, nice enough, brave enough. I never thought I was *anything* enough. I worried too much about competitors, rivals real and imagined, people who seemed to have better access to stories, more powerful contacts. I dissipated my own natural energy, wasted it. I didn't know how to relax. To meet the hurdles of the story process, to jump them, you have to believe in your ability to get the job done well. That belief is what overcomes insecurity. It's what makes you forget yourself so that you can be yourself.

$$\Diamond$$

HUGH DOWNS, the $1-million-a-year television personality from ABC–TV's "20/20" always seems relaxed, calm, and serene. But before he got to this point, he had to conquer an inferiority complex, what he once described to me in our interview as an "ugly duckling complex."

He told me that he used to hate to audition for jobs. He was self-conscious, was always clearing his throat. He thought his voice would fail him, that there was always someone better around, "someone with a metallic voice, punchier style." He was even scared of his own inflections, thinking they were weak when compared to someone else's.

Downs had a friend who saw him fumbling with himself. His friend gave him this advice: "Forget your voice. Think of what you're saying." This stopped Downs in his tracks. "It all boiled down to the difference between *what*

I'm doing and how I'm doing it. If you operate on the 'how' theory, you are looking in a mirror. But if you operate on the 'what' theory, you deal with the matter at hand. That is a matter of relaxation. I worried all the time about what the program executives would think of me. One day I decided this: 'I will do things the best way I know how. If I don't do them right, I don't belong here.'"

The minute Downs adopted that attitude, people came after him with jobs. His success was virtually assured. Downs discovered a great but simple truth—that people who dare to be their best selves attract positive reactions. A lot of people go through life thinking they have to make an impression. They do and usually it's the wrong kind. To be a showoff journalist is to care more about the *notion* of journalism than the *substance* of journalism. I have been scared in interviews, like when I interviewed President Jimmy Carter after he had been defeated by Ronald Reagan, when he was surrounded by a coterie of Secret Service men, politicians, and publicists, males huddled in his shadow. They listened intently while we talked, watching *their* man talk to a woman through amused facial expressions, seeing how *he* would handle *her* questioning. I didn't know if I would get the kind of story I had set out to get. At first I was distracted by his entourage. I felt self-conscious being in the presence of men wearing vested Ivy League suits, carrying holsters and wired with ear plugs. But I lost myself in that interview. I blocked out the scene and narrowed the vision of the moment down to Jimmy and me. I have come to trust the fact that I do an interview, a story, in a highly personal way, *my* way. Once I truly accepted the originality of me, I calmed down and began to do my best work.

When I discussed feelings of insecurity with Hugh Downs, he said: "One day I woke up to the fact that . . . all I had to do was be the best me. When I realized that I didn't need to compete, to worry about someone else, my days got better. There was always going to be someone better-looking. Someone with a better voice. But once I established myself as Hugh Downs, nobody was going to top me on that. That gave me a sense of security. There is no one more like Hugh Downs than Hugh Downs."

A strange silence hung between us. It puzzled Downs. He asked me if I understood what he meant. I told him I did.

THE TOP
OF THE HEAP

GAHAN WILSON once sketched a cartoon that summed up success in a wonderful scribble. It showed a strange creature, a cross between a goblin and a fat person, whose stubby legs seemed too close to the ground, looking up at a map that was nothing more than the craggy outline of a steep hill. The apex was marked "Top of the heap." The base was marked "Bottom of the heap." An arrow pointed to the bottom and carried a depressing message to the person surveying it: "You are *here,*" it intoned. The creature, filled with a common desire—success—looked at the map with bulging eyes, as if the terrible truth had suddenly dawned. The climb to the top, should it be attempted, was not going to be easy, and at the peak, the satisfaction would be brief.

Wilson, who had made it to the top, uses his own experiences as grist for cartoons which appear regularly in *The New Yorker, Playboy* and *Paris-Match.* He is an elegant man descended from William Jennings Bryant and P. T. Barnum, of circus fame. His late father, Allen Barnum Wilson, invented the venetian blind. He was born rich. But the family wealth was not placed at his disposal because his outrageous career choice—to be a cartoonist—was deemed a job unbefitting the name. He got neither family approval nor family money, and found himself on his own, a bohemian living in a Greenwich Village garret with no electricity and a view of nothing but other slums.

He worked hard and took his cartoons around to magazine editors who laughed heartily at them but said nobody would understand them. He was told his cartoons wouldn't sell. But these were the kinds of cartoons he wanted to do and he did them anyway. People geared toward success don't let go easily of their visions. But Wilson had to deal with a double sting: professional rejection and poverty. Poverty is one thing. The emotional part of rejection is quite another test, clawing and scratching your way along a flat land to get a little closer to the top. Wilson dared to go against the tide and won. Once, over a glass of champagne, I asked this man, now one of the great Hollywood talents who creates macabre characters for science fiction movies, about the joy of success. After all, I had never seen him do a cartoon that exemplified the sweetness of success. As a reply, he sketched an unforgettable cartoon in words.

"When I lived at the bottom rung of society, I had my telephone turned off because I didn't pay my bill. I got a postcard in lightning-bold print to shock me to attention. It read like a threat. I had the feeling that someone was coming to break down my door, stamp all over me with hobnail boots, kill my cat, take the telephone off the wall, and smack it in my face.

"Well, it's different when you're in the upper echelon, when you've dallied too long in the south of France and your accountant has been sloppy about paying your bills. All right, you've been disconnected—and I have been under just these circumstances. But it's different when you're well-to-do. You simply call and say, 'Sorry, I've been in France, my check is on the way,' and, like magic, your phone is turned back on."

There is the *other* side of Wilson's success. A Japanese artist friend, also struggling, invited him to dinner, a small stir-fry vegetable meal prepared in a wok. There was plenty of cheap wine and they were enjoying themselves when, without warning, a horrendous fight broke out in the next apartment. The walls were thin. A couple was fighting, yelling and screaming at each other. The din was shattered by a hard bang against the wall, as if a body had been hurled against it. Wilson's friend commented matter-of-factly, "It must be ghastly for ordinary people to live like this." Wilson agreed with his friend.

The supercilious attitude would seem, on the surface, to be obnoxious. But in reality it was a success attitude, the confidence of believing that their talent somehow made them extraordinary. They believed that their bottom-of-the-heap living was temporary, just a transient step in the climb to the top. They had focused sharply on the vision of themselves as successful artists. Wilson expressed his success strategy to me simply: "It takes a lot of brass to succeed. Your self-expectations have to be more powerful than the whole bloody world's rejection. You have to face adverse situations and say: 'I'm right, they're wrong.' And you have to believe it with all your heart."

Wilson told me about an art magazine that ran an important forecast column, a clearly defined barometer of important trends geared to help artists "sell" their work in the upcoming year. The evaluation was considered a bible. Once, during Wilson's lean years, when he wasn't selling and wishing he were, the magazine predicted childlike cartoons that had no detailed elaborations were "in." Wilson refused to do cartoons in that style. A few years went by and Wilson was still poor, still struggling and still not doing childlike cartoons. But he was beginning to sell a few cartoons for $2.50 apiece.

The writer of the column later ran one of Wilson's cartoons to illustrate an "odd" happening, an example of a distant comet that seemed to be catching on. Gahan had always been sure of his talent and his approach. What he wasn't sure of was whether or not it would succeed. "Along with the brass," he told me, "you've got to cross your fingers for good luck. When you have a contrary opinion, you must be prepared to brush off rejections. And you have to pray to God that it works out all right." I had a wonderful lunch with Gahan the day we talked. He ordered champagne and, later, burgundy wine ("Louis La-Tour . . . Meursault . . . 1978") and he asked me a personal question as a friend: Did I know what it felt like to be hungry? He asked because anybody who has experienced the gnawing feeling of physical hunger knows it's an added impetus to want to succeed.

$$\Diamond$$

ON A LAZY SUMMER evening in late June, during the mid-1950s, in a small, crowded Boston restaurant run by the Women's Educational and Industrial Union I was a "one" seated at a small table for two. The harried hostess, juggling a steady parade of customers, asked to seat another woman at my table, while actually doing so.

My unexpected companion was the prototypical Boston Proper. Tanned skin abused into deep creases by too much sun. Scrambled white hair, tinted a vague lavender. She wore a battered navy blue blazer, with a sailing insignia stitched on the left breast pocket. Clearly she was a boat person. Her expression was typically Brahmin, emotionless, except for Delft blue eyes that turned out to be gentler than I would have guessed.

After perfunctory chitchat, polite observations about the weather, a "Lovely evening, isn't it?" the woman ordered a steak dinner and I ordered a small salad, which was all I could afford. Then she made an extraordinarily kind gesture. She offered me one of her Parker House rolls, oven-warmed and invitingly aromatic. I was ashamed, a little, that she had seen hunger in my eyes.

In those lean years I normally spent my dinner allowance of twenty cents on tea and toast at a now-defunct

Howard Johnson's near the Boston University campus where, at night, I studied journalism, encouraged by a Professor Robert Baram, who periodically told me that I could be "good." I exaggerated his prediction in my mind because it was something I wanted to believe was within my grasp. And there I was, at a "real" restaurant where "real" food was being served, celebrating the professor's predictions by being able to spend two dollars for dinner, not the usual twenty cents.

I was there because of a free-lance story I had sold to the *Boston Globe,* a farfetched Sunday feature, about a chef who sculpted figures out of melted lamb fat. The *Globe* paid five dollars that I split with my mother, who urged me to spend my share on a "nice" dinner. This was success, being able to leave my grubby junior clerk-typist day job in a government office to eat in a restaurant. I slathered butter on the delicious Parker House roll, enjoying every morsel, eating it slowly, oblivious to everything except how good it tasted.

The waitress, who was wearing one of those starched, crochet-trimmed handkerchiefs bursting out of the bodice pocket of her uniform like a pseudo-corsage, arrived at the table with the lady's steak and my salad. She knew that the rolls came only with a complete dinner. She controlled a shriek that came out a loud harrumph and announced furiously that I was eating someone else's food. My dinner companion told the waitress she had offered me the roll, but the shame still stung me.

I have always associated having bread with being successful. Once, when I got a raise from Tom Winship, the *Globe* editor evaluating my work, he glibly said: "Yup, you deserve more bread." He never knew why I burst into nervous laughter. But that evening I walked out of the restaurant head held high, heart heavy. My immediate goal became to find a way to support myself so I would never again be denegrated in public. Like the creature in Gahan Wilson's cartoon, I was at the bottom of the heap.

◇

ONE OF THE MOST successful women I ever met was the late NBC–TV superstar, Jessica Savitch, who began her career as an awkward disc jockey. By age thirty-five, she had become a commanding television anchorwoman making in excess of $500,000 a year. We had met several times before her tragic death on October 24, 1983, when the car she and a friend, Martin Fischbein, a *New York Post* executive, were driving in ran off a restaurant driveway in New Hope, Pennsylvania, and plunged upside down in the muddy Delaware Canal.

The last time we met to talk, a year before the accident, it was in her up-on-high Rockefeller Plaza office. Savitch repeated to me something she had said to me before, something I cannot forget. "Success doesn't bring happiness," she said slowly, studying my reaction, as if trying out an idea on me. "Success brings success." This was the cool appraisal of a realist. She had said the same thing again and again to me for several years, while achieving *more* success. Savitch had not changed her mind.

When we talked, her door was shut. She had left orders not to be interrupted. She even told her secretary that she would accept no telephone calls unless the president was calling from the White House. She wasn't being pretentious. She really was expecting that call. A couple of years earlier, when we had met for the first time, Savitch, a lovely blond with a small, tight body, had asked "how come" I didn't appear jealous of her staggering broadcast salary? Jealousy was an automatic response from print journalists, she said, and she sensed I was different. At first I thought Savitch's question was too aggressive, nervy. But I answered her because I felt she was doing what I like to do in interviews: remove barriers, real or imagined. Besides, I liked her. I wanted to be friends.

I told Savitch that I had always fantasized that success would be an endorsement, a kind of personal insurance and that with it would come automatic respect. Oscar Levant, the late pianist, cracked to Alan Jay Lerner, the world-famous lyricist after good reviews: "What a great night for envy!" I once thought jealousy was a pleasant acknowledgment, the same as being noticed. I had no idea that the politics of professional jealousy can mangle, even kill a career. I told Savitch that, to me, jealousy conditions your abilities in a negative way, like blocking your best self under the debris of envy. I told her that I never squander my energies because to achieve success is to have single-mindedness of purpose. Mine was and is to be as good a journalist as I can be. I told her jealousy dilutes that power, and I know it was at that moment that she acknowledged me as a person, not someone who was there for a story. She, in fact, turned the tables on me, interviewing me, asking a series of point-blank questions that were intelligent, though delivered machine-gun style. I answered them because her curiosity was sincere, the budding of a friendship. She was trying to make the interior of me visible to her. Still, her questions took on the characteristics of a probe, as if she were judge and jury. Inside I smiled at the difference in our approach. She hit hard. I peeled away the layers slowly. We were two similar women who used different styles to arrive at the same spot.

Her first question was for me to define success. I told Savitch that I measured my success in terms of pride and self-expression first, that dollars were not one of my priorities. Then I laughed and told her that it was fantastic to have money to do some of the things you'd like to do, but money was never the hub of my pursuit. I told her I could afford a fine meal, taxis, good clothes, a house. That was enough. She smiled and from that moment on we talked as colleagues who respected one another's achievements. She asked more questions that made sense and I went along with her, knowing that she was playing my game of mutual discovery, seeing for herself if I was sensitive enough, caring enough to answer the same kinds of questions I would be putting to her. She sat behind her desk, manicured hands folded neatly on top of a small stack of letters waiting to be signed, letters sitting next to a box of makeup, hair brushes, and a magnifying mirror. Did I feel, she asked, that people who are successful tend to take risks, do or try to do what they're told cannot be done? She already knew the answer so I told her about Maureen Reagan, President Reagan's daughter from his first wife, Jane Wyman. Maureen once told me she doesn't close matchbook covers before striking them just because that's what the tag orders. Her tiny rebellion was symptomatic of a larger daring, an attitude that translates into the success strategy of sticking your neck out, daring to break rules to achieve an objective, knowing, of course, you could be burned.

Savitch smiled then, that wonderful mystery smile of contained amusement with which she often closed her news broadcasts. She asked if I had ink in my veins rather than blood. Savitch was using an old newspaper line about people who view journalism as a religion. She knew that by using language familiar to me I would understand that what she was actually asking was if I had ever considered doing a job other than journalism.

I told Savitch about a man I knew who wanted to be an actor. His father suggested he could try the stage, try Hollywood, try television, but it would be better to have a practical job that offered "security," say as an electrician or a house painter. The man told me he always felt that if he had something to fall back on, he might actually fall because "security" might make him complacent. He likened it to being a high-wire trapeze artist who worked without a net. "If you have a net, you might use it," he told me. "If you don't have a net, you concentrate on *not* slipping."

Savitch asked what motivated me in the beginning, what made me think I *could* be successful? I told her what welled up inside me was a strong, steady desire to better myself, better my situation. Eventually I imagined success

in specific terms. Earning seventy-five dollars a week. Fin-
ishing my journalism courses. Eating properly. Never having to wear stockings with runs in them. I was nowhere
near those goals and there weren't any signposts pointing
me along the way. I was sure I was going to do it.

After she got her interview I got mine.

What was bothering Savitch were the demands of success, the pull between being a fighter and not becoming
arrogant in the process. Savitch worried about what all
successful people, and particularly women, worry about:
Is it possible to be liked and to be successful? Does one
cancel out the other? Savitch, who was actually doing a
needlepoint as we spoke with the phrase, "Don't Mistake
Kindness for Weakness," had set a cutoff point on the subject of niceness: "When people take advantage of my kindness," she said, "or when my kindness is not taken seriously,
that happens only once. That person gets one chance."
Savitch never wanted to be perceived as vulnerable but,
without these systematic defenses, she was. Success could
never really insulate her sensitivities, and although she
didn't know it, that was what gave her beauty dimension.

We talked about the ultimate success being a package,
being able to strike a balance between personal success
and career—loving someone and loving what you do and
not having one detract from the other. That's when Savitch
fell into a sad silence. She divorced her first husband, Mel
Korn, a Philadelphia advertising executive in 1980, after
ten months of marriage. She found her second husband,
gynecologist Dr. Donald Rollie Payne, hanged in the base-
ment of their Washington home, an apparent suicide, after
five months of marriage. When I read one of Savitch's obit-
uary stories, she had reportedly told friends that her relationship with Fischbein, who died with her, was so good
that she was thinking maybe there was something in life
besides work success, after all.

She never got to find out for sure. She had gotten only
to the point of realizing there's a false side to success.

Savitch knew something important was missing. I always thought that Savitch felt she would never be a total success without a successful relationship with a man. She almost had it with Fischbein, the man who died with her. But I also knew she wouldn't substitute marriage for career, that marriage would have to be an adjunct. I remember her resoluteness well: "I wouldn't give up what I'm doing for anything," she said. "I'd only be willing to make adjustments. Even sacrifices. But if it came to a choice, no, there would be no choice."

Then she looked me straight in the eye. "Are you ambitious?" she asked. "Yes." "Ambition is a word I hate," she said as if ashamed of her own. "It's not a positive word when applied to women." I told Savitch that, to me, ambition was a positive power, that what we were really talking about is excellence, that terrific feeling that the job you're doing is being done as well as it can be done. Savitch, a "nice" woman, then asked me if I thought nice women were thought of as pushovers. I told her that the most successful people I knew were the kindest ones, that those who had rooms at the top were usually the most decent.

$$\Diamond$$

THERE IS A POINT in everyone's career, for most not until mid-life, when you become aware of your mortality. You realize that time is the most precious commodity you've got. Suddenly, it seems that everything you do, everything you achieve, is for nothing. But, conversely, since time is of the essence, everything is important, everything counts. Even the failures become part of the fabric of success.

Today friends call people like me "success slaves." I focused singlemindedly on success. I made judicious use of my time. The older I get, the more I need to know why the success strive overwhelmed everything in my life. Tennessee Williams referred to it as "the catastrophe of Success." False adulation. Jealousy. Friends that turned out to be phony. I hear more and more people today say they'd rather be happy than successful. They already know that one is not the same as the other. I hear these people, nonslaves, say that raises are fine but that, if they had a choice, they'd rather be "happy" on the job. But on the other hand, success is not totally satisfying. You wonder if there isn't something else. Some sort of missing link. You want "other things" when you achieve success. Someone to love one-to-one. The security of a few dependable friends. And this has nothing to do with career success.

I made this admission to Los Angeles-based Dr. Thomas Noguchi, the Japanese-born coroner and author of the controversial autopsy book, *Coroner,* the man who did the autopsies on celebrities like Marilyn Monroe and Robert F. Kennedy. In my interview with him in November, 1983, the doctor told me that he, too, had shut everything out of his life except work, as if "possessed" by it. What drove him was a primary urge to live up to the expectations of his father, also a doctor. I told Dr. Noguchi my success was the opposite extreme, that I did not live up to my father's expectations because they were so limited. He asked me what Jessica Savitch had asked, what all successful people ask at one time or another: "Do you think success is all that it is cracked up to be?" "No," I said, "do you?"

Eight years earlier, while Dr. Noguchi was doing an autopsy on a man his age, his build, it struck him that he could and someday *would* be the man on the slab. That day, when he went back to his office, he played a little game with himself.

"Suppose," he said, "you were told you had twenty-four hours to live. What would you consider important? Your career? No. Your celebrity? No. What then? *Me.* What really counts is *me.*" Dr. Noguchi was not describing narcissism. He was talking about the importance of balancing the consuming sensation of success with all the other aspects of a full life, right down to the smallest details.

That day, Noguchi walked out of his office, told no one where he was going. He went jogging. He went supermarket shopping. He telephoned a brother in Japan. Before seriously considering his death, he believed there was no time to do the little things he wanted to do. When he thought about death as his permanent disappearance, a state of transit which he described as "nonnegotiable," his attitude changed. He had gotten past his success, past thinking that success, like life, would last forever.

Dr. Noguchi convinced me that I could do things for myself, things that were simply pleasurable, and my success wouldn't vanish because of it. When you loosen your hold on success, when it ceases to be your master, success becomes more comfortable.

John B. Coleman is the famous hotel entrepreneur whose luxury hotels, including the New York Ritz-Carlton, are reportedly worth more than $200 million. When he was seventeen, he applied for a passport and discovered he was adopted. It was a shock that took immediate effect and lasted a long time. He fought his feelings of insecurity by establishing an identity as a business tycoon. But what he really wanted, peace of mind, had absolutely nothing to do with fame and fortune.

He felt isolated, had no sense of "belonging." His fantastic business success improved his lifestyle. But it didn't make him feel wonderful about himself. He began putting up barriers to thwart new hurts that looked to him like old hurts. He wasn't defensive a little. He was defensive a lot. "Defense shut *everything* out," he said, "especially the chance of success. I learned to open myself up and let the real world come in. It was not as painful as leaving the world out."

Coleman was and is a worldly success. But he had too many unrealistic expectations about success. He thought an image of business strength would make him feel strong inside, make up for the voids in his personal life. It didn't. His mistake was in assuming that having success would make up for other things he wanted and never got. Success is not a substitute for anything else. Success makes your life successful. That's a lot. But that's all. Coleman went into outpatient psychotherapy at the Menninger Clinic in Topeka, Kansas, for eighteen months to find this out.

$$\diamond$$

MY SUCCESS is deceptively simple. I made it past my conditioning. There is a kind of person who craves success and is willing to give up something to get it. I am that person. But I also know that success has an innate insatiability to it. I didn't know it when I began, but the more success you get, the more you want. And I had no idea how dear the price of success is in terms of spending yourself to get it. You have to be obsessed with your goals, shutting out people and interruptions to concentrate primarily on what you want to do.

When the late Ingrid Bergman had undergone two mastectomies and, at age sixty-three, was still taking chemotherapy, we met in New York at the Hotel Pierre for tea. It was late October, 1980, and we talked about consistent drive, the one most necessary element of success. Bergman told me that her drive had caused deep chasms in all her marriages—particularly the last one to Swedish producer, Lars Schmidt, from whom she had been divorced six years earlier. She told me that, regardless of the outcome, she never put a lid on her drive. "In some ways," she said, "I was selfish . . . when the opportunities came, I could have said no. I could have said my husband, this one or that one [the children] need me. I could have said I should not be separated from my children. But I didn't say no. I said *yes*. And that was selfish. . . ." I asked her if she had regrets. "The sharpest force in my life has always been acting. I love it now as I did when I was eighteen," she said. Bergman had made career success her priority, regardless of the consequences to her marriage.

The pursuit of success goes against the grain of traditional Puritan upbringing. You are taught to put others before yourself. Successful people do not do that. They center all their energies on their goals. The good side of selfishness within this context is that when you answer only to yourself, you are *free* to pursue success without distraction. I never stopped to consider the balance of a personal life. I equated success with the independence of answering to no one. Then I found out I had no one. Aloneness doesn't seem bad in retrospect, when it's seen in the glow and recognition of success. But the actual moments of aloneness and struggle are bitter. What saved me during these down times was telling myself everything was going to be all right, that I'd make it. I *pretended* everything was fine. I thought if I acknowledged the possibility of failure, I'd invite it. I fooled myself.

A few years into college and career, a fine UPI wire-service reporter proposed marriage, promising he would give me what I so clearly wanted for myself: success. He telephoned me one evening at 10:00 P.M. when he knew I had just come in from my Boston University classes. He said he had to see me, that he was on his way, that it couldn't wait. Half an hour later we were sitting together on the porch, in the dark, in side-by-side rocking chairs, not even holding hands. This man made an impassioned little love speech, not knowing that his love was unrequited. Marriage was not a priority of mine. He asked me what I wanted, that whatever it was, he would give it to me. It was one of those wild promise-her-anything approaches—flattering but totally unrealistic. I told him that I wanted to be a journalist, something only I could give myself. An awful silence divided us and I know the man cried because he sniffled into a handkerchief, gently dabbing his eyes as I gave him my answer. Without hesitation, I told him his success would be his success and my success, which I didn't have then, would be mine. Still he hugged me and kissed my cheek before he left. The next year I read his wedding announcement in the paper and I was glad he was making a life for himself.

Ten years later, he showed up, unannounced, at my *Globe* desk. I had not seen him since the night of his proposal. He said he came to congratulate me. He had watched my progress, read my stories. He even told me I had written some of the stories he would like to have written. He implied that there were times he thought I had beaten him in terms of stories that had news value. He was the best loser I've ever known.

Just before leaving, he told me he had married and had three babies. Looking hard at me, he asked if my baby was journalism and did that satisfy me. Before I had a chance to answer, he then asked me if I felt that I had "missed out" on an important chapter of my life. Without waiting for my reply, he quickly bent down, kissed me on the cheek, and left my office in what blurred into one sole movement. I haven't seen him since. I always wished that I told him that I felt good about what I was doing—that I express my passions in my stories. But I know that's not what he wanted to hear. That was why he left so quickly. Maybe I knew all along that finding the right mate was one of life's biggest struggles, and if I had to choose between finding the right career and finding the right man, I'd choose the work.

Consciously or unconsciously, I limited my own vision, as if warning myself to keep my eye on my objective, not to stray. I assumed tunnel vision on purpose. I realized none of this until the struggles were over, and I came out on the side of success. Then I looked back and was shocked to see how obsessed I had been with journalism, with the business of turning my life around, with proving my own potential and worth. I had blocked everything and everyone out. I was astonished at the steep price of success and how willingly I had paid it. The terrible truth was that I had no trusted friends to confide in, no one to whom I could explain how I felt about what I had done.

Success has its obvious drawbacks in romantic situations. The opposite sex doesn't really understand a woman's desire to succeed. Modern men pay lip service to successful women. They *say* they admire them. But if a woman's success is equal to a man's success, somehow he feels demeaned. Career success slowly corrodes man-woman relationships, especially if the demands and rewards of her success interfere with his. Equal success or, worse, a woman who is more successful than a man, brings on a kind of subtle competition that can destroy a relationship. It is usually the woman who compromises.

Alan Alda, the millionaire actor, is an ardent feminist. But his married life contradicts his espousal about liberated women. His wife, Arlene, has been married to him for twenty-four years and she's a startling contrast to her husband's glamorous co-stars, women like Loretta Swit and Meryl Streep. I met the Aldas in May, 1981. *He* was exactly the Alan Alda of "MASH." *She* was a lovable, gentle, old-fashioned woman who wore no makeup except a dab of lipstick. She patted her husband's cheek in a gesture of affection that suggested a mother-child bond. And when they were being photographed together, she didn't want to stand side-by-side. *She* insisted that *he* sit. She stood behind him in a kind of charmingly Victorian pose. It was a symbol of her role as wife and keeper.

During the interview, she made it clear that her husband came first, that his career came first, that she was his anchor, his "support." She talked of "managing" him, especially when the pressure of work made him sullen and grouchy. She was a woman who catered to her man, coddled him through the tensions of success.

I couldn't help myself. I asked her if she "mothered" her husband? This woman, who graduated Phi Beta Kappa from New York's Hunter College and had played clarinet with the Houston Symphony Orchestra, answered: "Yes, sometimes . . . yes." Her success was a marriage success. What she put into the relationship, all her energy and all her love, netted her a *unity* with her man. She glowed with that kind of success. It was apparent that her husband adored her. She had what she wanted.

When I left the Aldas, I realized, again, that successful men usually don't marry equally successful women. They marry women who are content to be wives, women who will look after them. Successful men want *traditional* women who will be noncompetitive, women to run their homes and bear their babies. They want women like my mother.

My mother was a breathtakingly beautiful woman with fine, chiseled features. She had great charm and a visionary mind. She was also a numbers whiz with a flair for business economics, and a keen judge of people and situations, a problem-solver who could envision the possibilities of any given situation. She had the ability to execute crisis decisions. I remember how she had given my father sound business advice many times, pointing out flaws in contracts, naming people he shouldn't trust. He pooh-poohed her reactions, preferring to follow his own instincts that led him into financial disasters.

My mother could have been my father's business partner, his most trusted adviser. But he looked at her as a mere *woman*. How often I overheard and secretly resented his philosophy of keeping his business to himself: "I don't believe you should let your right hand know what your left hand is doing," he said, destroying what could have been a great mutuality. He forfeited my mother's wisdom and brainpower on the basis of her vibrant femaleness, her dazzling prettiness. I promised myself this would never happen to me. But it was happening everywhere to millions of women. My mother was a fantastically successful woman in a way I could never be, a behind-the-scenes heroine who brought up four children, insisting they be, first, good people and then good at whatever jobs they chose. She was successful at one of the hardest jobs in the world: mothering.

She hardly ever used the word success. But my mother insisted that we never waste precious time. "Accomplished people use time to their advantage" is the theory she drummed into my head. If you watched television, you didn't just watch television. You had to "do something" with your hands simultaneously. You hemmed hemlines. You sewed buttons. You darned socks. My mother conditioned me to be disciplined, to make the best use of time. I did, but I did it in a different way.

$$\diamondsuit$$

THERE HAVE been other factors that led me toward an obsession with success. Twenty years ago, my ten-day unconsummated marriage was terminated in a court of law. I had a brush with potential violence on my Nassau honeymoon. The man I married, impotent, threatened to throw me off a hotel balcony, actually pressing me hard against the railing, bending me backward. This is the man who had courted me passionately for months, always lovingly called me "princess," wrote me an amorous love letter every day from the first day we met. He was the man who bought me glamorous see-through black lace lingerie and sent me bouquets of bird of paradise flowers. I escaped his frustrated rage only because distant voices in the background seemed to be getting closer and he released me. I faced the judge wearing a blue silk chemise dress from my trousseau.

For a long time after my honeymoon, any man who touched me casually in any gesture of friendship was surprised at the way I jumped—I was tense and nervous. I had gone into the marriage a virgin at a time when virginity was still prized and premarital sex unacceptable, and that's the way I left it. I also left behind me a new house filled with new furniture. I asked for nothing except my freedom and the use of my own name again. I came home to my mother and to a small mountain of unopened presents, which I returned. Also waiting for me was a Bachrach set of proofs of a church celebration and reception frozen by dozens of camera clicks. Maybe I should have discarded the proofs, but I had them made up into a beautiful wedding album. I still have fantasies about the proverbial knight in shining armor, the one man who'll care enough about me to make up for a lost honeymoon. It would be wonderful to have old longings filled. I also know no one is ever going to do that. No one can.

Success carries with it a certain discipline that comes in handy in times of woe. Emotional pain can be a source of self-discovery. The day I left the courthouse free was a happy day, and my desire to have career success was more overwhelming than ever. Marital success was not to be mine but the alternate chance to be recognized, admired for the qualities that make me *me* was as a journalist. I didn't know it then but the attitude of wanting to move past my personal failure was the beginning of my most meaningful success.

In retrospect, I can define my attitude more precisely. I wanted people to have a good opinion of me but it had to be justified. I would have to earn it. I was greedier than ever about wanting to succeed. My marriage was a failure. I wanted to *do* things, achieve, be singled out as special because of my work. It was silly but I had the attitude: "I'm going to show them," and this small determination gave me resilience. I decided to work harder than ever. I saw it as a way toward self-redemption. T. S. Eliot once said: "Nothing dies harder than the desire to think well of yourself." There are no real failures, only unsuccessful ventures. How well I remember the exact moment I let go of what was left of my marriage, the thing I had hung onto most. I threw all my love letters into a roaring fireplace on a winter day eighteen months later when a blizzard prevented my going to the office. I don't know why, but I had the urge to reach under my bed into a tin box where I had hidden the letters and burn them. It felt wonderful to watch them disintegrate into ashes. I had burned my bridges. The trouble is, I didn't know how much patience, time, and energy it would take to build new ones.

◊

SUCCESS IS very sweet, the reward of excellence. It's a good thing not to pursue an objective with the idea of great monetary rewards. They can come anyway, the by-product of good work. When you pursue a goal for the love of it that, in itself, is a kind of success. One of the greatest success strategies is based on the act of listening to your own urges, following your instincts. It's the making of a maverick. The most successful people I have met have considered the impact of their imagination. They have done what they have loved to do even though people have tried to talk them out of it. A goal can lose its fascination if it's based solely on a desire for materialistic growth. Acquiring things is nice but not totally satisfying as getting people to think the way you do. Success can be measured in terms of influence as well as dollars. Ralph Lauren, the millionaire designer, has both. But he discovered another truth: Complacency is the beginning of the rotting process. It can disrupt the process of success.

The last time I interviewed Lauren, the forty-two-year-old designer, he was sitting in his denlike New York office wearing old jeans and an open-collared shirt. He had on shoes—loafers—but no socks. It was a cold September day in 1983, and Lauren had a cold. He could have kept warm in one of his cashmere sweaters but he had wrapped himself like a papoose in an old Sante Fe afghan. Lauren, a designer who preaches tradition in a world hell-bent on change, told me that day that he measures success in terms of how he feels about himself. I didn't believe him at first and I countered with the two big numbers behind his name: $450 million annual volume in clothes, furnishings, cosmetics and the $10.5 million spent annually in ads in which he appears. He, like Jessica Savitch, then asked my idea of success. I told him that success should not only be measured in achievement but also in what obstacles you had to overcome to get there. Lauren, a former tie salesman who now drives a custom-built Porsche, lives in a Fifth Avenue duplex overlooking Central Park, and has homes in East Hampton, Jamaica, and a 6,000-acre ranch in Colorado, smiled at me and said: "Exactly." Then he told me this story:

"Some people are motivated from the beginning by financial success. I've always wanted to be a success inside. To do that, you have to love what you do and do what you love. That's *purified* motivation. To succeed financially is nice, but it's not magical.

"Most people think that what they love has to be put away and what they *have* to do is work. It's the same attitude as believing a medicine will do good only if it tastes bad. The most successful people are those who go to work and say: 'Jeez, I love this.'

"At an early period of my career, I made wide neckties. I went to a major store and the buyer, a Bostonian, said he'd buy them if I'd agree to sell them under the private label of the store and narrow them. I said: 'No.' I loved wide ties.

"You have to believe in yourself even when they close the door. I needed that order, the money. But I felt I was right. My goal was true self-expression, not dollars. Six months later, that buyer called to say: 'Hey, we'll do it your way.'

"I trust my gut feelings about everything. Instinct is something we all have. It's a voice that comes from somewhere in your stomach. It tells you if you're right or wrong. But sometimes you rationalize that voice away. You fool yourself. In the end, it's you talking to you. You've got to trust your own hunches.

"I picked the president of my company, Peter Strom, against the advice of experts. He's a low-key guy, doesn't come on like dynamite. He's got the kind of personality that grows on you. He's not a one-shot personality, someone who immediately convinces you he's going to take over the world. I had interviewed other worldly men who came on strong, made witty wisecracks. I picked him. I went with my gut feelings of feeling good about him.

"That was seven years ago. We had a $12 million annual volume. Today, it's $450 million. The experts asked me what I saw in this guy. I told them: 'He's the kind I'd like to say hello to every morning, someone you know will be on your side, no matter what. That's saying a lot.'

"I've failed. But failure is just a passage. You go down. You get up. I went from being a genius to a nongenius. Nine years ago, my company started dwindling. I didn't have a strong support system. The cash flow was tight. I felt squeezed. I could have gone out of business. I wasn't bankrupt, but it was getting dark. I shivered. People I trusted in the company—they left me.

"On one rainy morning, I was getting dressed to go to the office. I hated to go to the office in those days. But I wanted to show people that I still had my head up, despite it all. It was a very symbolic gesture, but I reached for a white suit that day. It was raining outside of me and inside of me. But the white suggested sunniness. You wear black to a funeral. You wear white to a party. I said to myself, 'I reached for something white, something sunny and bright. I can't go around crumbling in the dark. I've got to go in there and fight.' From that day forward, things got better. I think it's how you perceive things. How you take the worst things and make them better."

$$\diamond$$

WHAT WE ALWAYS forget and I learn over and over again in my interviews is the price of success. How it can burden celebrities with unrealistic expectations, as if celebrities were deified beings who don't bleed the way we do. I visited Bette Davis in her dressing room backstage at the Lunt-Fontanne Theatre in September of 1974 when she was sixty-six and she expressed a common yearning which we don't usually associate with successful people: loneliness. I asked her what she did when she was lonely? I thought she'd say she would call a friend, "Dahling, I polish the silvah," she said and raised one eyebrow menacingly, studying my reaction to what could be considered an arrogant answer. Then, without the prodding of another question, she voluntarily explained herself while munching, of all things, a tuna salad sandwich with pickles. "As we get older," she drawled in that inimitable voice, "and have more successes, there are fewer and fewer people with whom to spend time. When you're famous, you have to *act* famous. That's an effort. In the end, all you want to do is have a chat with someone who sees beyond the footlights."

When you are a public success, your "chat" is as public as your actions, as Joan Kennedy found out when she decided to face the press by "chatting" about her problems with alcohol with "friends," the press, who, of course, could not *see* beyond the footlights since she was then still the wife of Massachusetts Senator Edward Kennedy. This may have been one of Joan's greatest success moments, facing up to her fight against alcoholism, brought on by Edward Jr.'s cancer and leg amputation, the indelibility of Chappaquiddick, and her husband's quest for the presidency despite two Kennedy assassinations. It was December 5, 1979, and Joan, hands trembling, staged a press conference for a handful of journalists in her Boston apartment, describing her trials as "a little bit of hell." I always thought she was expressing the spirit of success when she said, "The *good* news is that I am successfully recovering from alcoholism. The result is that I feel I am a brand-new person. I have back my old confidence. I have a wonderful love of life."

The assembled press, a few national wire service reporters, and writers from local newspapers, acted as if Kennedy, who attended Manhattanville College of the Sacred Heart, was being too Pollyannaish. One of them asked why she had left Washington, suggesting by innuendo that she had abandoned her family. "I left, pure and simply, because

I was a very sick lady. I needed to try a new treatment program. . . ." One asked why she didn't try the programs in Washington. She said she had tried several, and in an almost-inaudible voice, admitted: "I had failed." Later she would say: "If I didn't get well, I'd have nothing else." She talked about joining Alcoholics Anonymous, about having the courage to go to a psychiatrist three times a week, about depending on friends. I know one thing for sure about success: Only the most successful people admit their failures. Success gives you the security of knowing you moved beyond your failures, as if you crossed the bridge of yourself and can look back and say: "I was *there* . . . look where I am now!"

This was an exciting moment for Joan Kennedy, a moment of personal victory, and she tried to play it down by being casual, almost folksy. She offered coffee to her "friends," the press. Even her choice of clothes implied informality: salt-and-pepper tweed jacket tossed over a black cowl-neck sweater and gray flannel trousers. Still the press had a hard-core attitude. She was on the hot seat, casual attitude or not. She was asked how it felt to be "number two" in the senator's life, "number one" being his career. She blushed: "I am not 'number two'," she said. "Ask Ted Kennedy." Then, sighing, she had the guts to admit the truth: "I'll never be 'number two' again."

She told the press that she had discovered how to recognize the pressures of celebrity, how to strike a balance in her life. She said her concept of professional success was to teach music to young children and music appreciation to their parents. One of the last things she said was: "I am not a militant feminist. I believe the most exciting thing about it [feminism] is that women today have a choice of having a career or staying at home." Kennedy has since made her choices. In the spring of 1981 she graduated from Lesley College. In late 1983 she was divorced from her husband of twenty-one years, the father of her three children. She doesn't have a job. She isn't married. Her success is personal. She has picked up the pieces of her life and gone on. She has proved herself to her self.

You can never say failure or setbacks are a good thing. Joan Kennedy's alcoholism was, in a sense, a failure to cope. But, once admitted, her failure is what became the crux of her success. She openly admitted her alcoholism. She said to herself, her family, her doctor, her friends, and, in the end, to the world: "I was an alcoholic but I've done something about it." There are all kinds of successes beyond career.

$$\Diamond$$

NEW YORK Mayor Edward I. Koch, son of poor Polish immigrants, sees success as a form of silent revenge, the perfect way to squelch detractors who cannot accomplish what he has accomplished—but would like to. I interviewed Koch on April 2, 1984, in Boston, over coffee at the Ritz-Carlton Hotel. It was a success scene with Hollywood overtones and the star, Mayor Koch, a trained lawyer, talked about his favorite subject, himself. Former Chicago Mayor Jane Byrne happened to be at the next table and couldn't help but eavesdrop, with obvious interest. Three of Koch's bodyguards sat at an adjoining table, keeping watch, while Koch personally tape-recorded me interviewing him.

Koch had just published his book, *Mayor,* which had become an overnight bestseller. His literary talents were described by Gay Talese in the *New York Times* as funny and "biting in a Mel Brooks sort of way."

I asked the mayor about the joy of his dual success, made more heady because he published the book against the advice of friends who told him to wait until he was out of office. What the mayor told me is what no one else ever admitted to me: that being a famous author was a wonderful revenge, a kind of "getting back" at people who had attacked him, reporters who think of themselves as real writers but never had a bestseller. He saw this success as victory over enemies.

"I've been constantly criticized by six New York reporters," the mayor told me. "Every one of them has written a book. I'm a good mayor. But I've beat six reporters in their own profession. For them, it must be unbearable." When he uttered the word *unbearable* it was from a wide smile that narrowed his eyes into slits. "I'm not getting even," he continued. "I'm getting ahead. John F. Kennedy once said it's a good idea to forgive your enemies and never forget their names. I never forget and I rarely forgive."

Koch's freedom of expression is related to his success. He can be blunt and get away with it. I asked him why he didn't edit his remarks, be more of the classic politician. In so many words he said that because he is a successful politician, he doesn't have to speak out of both sides of his mouth to please the opposites of his constituency. "Being blunt," he told me, "doesn't have to mean bad. It means: 'Listen, this is what I'm thinking.' " Koch's success allows him the privilege of speaking his mind, and, whether or not his audience agrees, his approach is construed to be "honest." Koch told me that honesty was the rock on which he built his success, that whether you asked his position on any given topic in public or private, his stand is the same. He had "dependable" opinions that reflected on his overall dependability. "If you are dealing with problems," he said, "it is best to do it honestly. It's a lot like dealing with cancer. People think if they don't discuss cancer it will go away. You have to use surgery to eliminate cancer." The surgery the mayor used was his tongue, a reputation that earned him the nickname "Mayor Mouth," only now he had put his words on paper and had become a national celebrity.

◇

SOMETIMES IN LIFE you have to decide you want to be a success more than anything. You might not call it success. It might simply be following the urges of your heart and soul. You are doing something that you *have* to do and you're giving it all you've got in terms of energy and dedication. Then something happens to stop you, an obstacle real or imagined. You are at a crossroad. Either you accept the obstacle as an insurmountable roadblock or you can figure a way to get around it. Willie Stargell, forty-three, had once faced that kind of choice. He told me about it one day in April, 1984, as we talked about his climb from a childhood in a housing project in Alameda, California, to his 1979 World Series championship as first baseman and team captain of the Pittsburgh Pirates. Stargell, born on a Seminole Indian reservation in Oklahoma, had retired in 1982 after twenty years in the National League. But he could have been stopped early when he was in the minors, a promising rookie en route to a ballgame at a Texas park. This is exactly what Stargell told me:

"Once you decide on a path, obstacles are going to float in your path unexpectedly. That's when it's easy to lose your enthusiasm. You need patience to deal with setbacks. When I started playing baseball, it was like God said to me: 'I'm going to create certain situations to see how you deal with them.' I'm talking about serious situations, like life-threatening situations.

"When I first started playing basebell, I was on my way to a ballpark in Texas and when I got to the player's entrance, two guys in trench coats came up to me. It was a real hot day and I should have known something was happening. One guy put a shotgun to my forehead and said: 'If you play tonight, nigger, you're going to get your brains blown out.'

"That was the great crossroad of my life. I had a *choice.* To play or not to play. I knew I didn't want to go back to the housing projects where I'd come from. My parents had worked two jobs each to create a better life for me. And baseball was what I loved, what I wanted to do. So I made up my mind. I said: 'Willie, if you're going to lose your life, do it playing baseball. But first I had to settle my kidneys down. My nervous system was all riled up. They seemed to be standing up on my head. I was very frightened. Devastated. That day was one of the best days for me on the field. But a couple of times I thought I heard a car backfire and I thought: 'Oh boy, this is it.' But I never heard from those two guys again. From that I learned this: If you love what you do and you want to do it, let nothing or nobody stop you."